Teaching Science Thinking

Teach your students how to think like scientists. This book shows you practical ways to incorporate science thinking in your classroom using simple "Thinking Tasks" that you can insert into any lesson. What is science thinking and how can you possibly teach and assess it? How is science thinking incorporated into the Next Generation Science Standards (NGSS) and how can it be woven into your curriculum? This book answers these questions.

This practical book provides a clear, research-verified framework for helping students develop scientific thinking as required by the NGSS. Your students will not be memorizing content but will become engaged in the real work scientists do, using critical thinking patterns such as:

◆ Recognizing patterns,
◆ Inventing new hypotheses based on observations,
◆ Separating causes from correlations,
◆ Determining relevant variables and isolating them,
◆ Testing hypotheses, and
◆ Thinking about their own thinking and the relative value of evidence.

The book includes a variety of sample classroom activities and rubrics, as well as frameworks for creating your own tools. Designed for the busy teacher, this book also shows you quick and simple ways to add deep science thinking to existing lessons.

Christopher Moore is the Dr. George F. Haddix Community Chair in Physical Science and associate professor of physics education at the University of Nebraska Omaha, USA. He is also the author of *Creating Scientists: Teaching and Assessing Science Practice for the NGSS*.

Also Available from Routledge
Eye On Education
www.routledge.com/eyeoneducation

Creating Scientists:
Teaching and Assessing Science Practice for the NGSS
Christopher Moore

STEM by Design: Strategies and Activities for Grades 4–8
Anne Jolly

The STEM Coaching Handbook:
Working with Teachers to Improve Instruction
Terry Talley

DIY Project Based Learning for ELA and History
Heather Wolpert-Gawron

DIY Project Based Learning for Math and Science
Heather Wolpert-Gawron

Write, Think, Learn: Tapping the Power of Daily Student Writing
Across the Content Areas
Mary K. Tedrow

Writing Science Right
Strategies for Teaching Scientific and Technical Writing
Sue Neuen and Elizabeth Tebeaux

Rigor in the Classroom: A Toolkit for Teachers
Barbara R. Blackburn

Teaching Science Thinking
Using Scientific Reasoning in the Classroom
Christopher Moore

Teaching Science Thinking

Using Scientific Reasoning in the Classroom

Christopher Moore

Routledge
Taylor & Francis Group

NEW YORK AND LONDON

First published 2019
by Routledge
52 Vanderbilt Avenue, New York, NY 10017

and by Routledge
2 Park Square, Milton Park, Abingdon, Oxon, OX14 4RN

Routledge is an imprint of the Taylor & Francis Group, an informa business

Library of Congress Cataloging-in-Publication Data
Names: Moore, Christopher (Professor) author.
Title: Teaching science thinking : using scientific reasoning in the
    classroom / Christopher Moore.
Description: New York, NY : Routledge, 2019. | Includes
    bibliographical references.
Identifiers: LCCN 2018033799 (print) | LCCN 2018047292 (ebook) |
    ISBN 9781315298634 (e-book) | ISBN 9781138237957 (hbk) |
    ISBN 9781138237964 (pbk) | ISBN 9781315298634 (ebk)
Subjects: LCSH: Teaching—Methodology. | Science—Methodology. |
    Critical thinking—Study and teaching.
Classification: LCC LB1025.3 (ebook) | LCC LB1025.3 .M655 2019
    (print) | DDC 371.102—dc23
LC record available at https://lccn.loc.gov/2018033799

ISBN: 978-1-138-23795-7 (hbk)
ISBN: 978-1-138-23796-4 (pbk)
ISBN: 978-1-315-29863-4 (ebk)

Typeset in Palatino
by Apex CoVantage, LLC

In memory of Dr. Rex Adelberger.

Contents

About the Author

Christopher Moore is the Dr. George F. Haddix Community Chair in Physical Science and associate professor of physics education at the University of Nebraska Omaha. Holding a M.S. in applied physics and a Ph.D. in chemistry from Virginia Commonwealth University, Dr. Moore has worked as a physical science teacher at several secondary schools in Virginia, as a professional materials scientist, and as a scholar of and consultant on science education. His education research focuses on the development of scientific reasoning and expert-like science practice abilities, with emphasis on practices that cross disciplines. He is author of the book *Creating Scientists: Teaching and Assessing Science Practice for the NGSS*, as well as dozens of articles for scholarly and practitioner journals. He has developed pre- and in-service teacher training workshops on scientific reasoning for school districts across the USA and internationally.

Dr. Moore's website is www.creatingscientists.com, where useful tools associated with this book can be found.

Acknowledgements

Nearly every scientist can credit at least one person that profoundly influenced their decision to pursue science. That person for me was physics professor Dr. Rex Adelberger. Rex was my freshman advisor at Guilford College in North Carolina many, many years ago. I entered Guilford planning to study athletic training. I left Guilford a physicist, and it was all Rex's fault. Rex is why I have degrees in physics, and his positive effect on my life is fundamentally why I eventually went into science education. It took him a few weeks to drag me away from a sports science major my freshman year. His shear stubbornness knew no bounds. For switching majors, I was rewarded with a D for content and an F for presentation on my first laboratory report. Somehow, I still wanted to get up every morning for an 8 AM class. The man taught me how to write in a very short amount of time. He baked muffins on Fridays, but only allowed those of us wearing a tie to partake in a failed attempt to make us couth. He once literally threw a book at me. He marked my left hand with an X every morning in class because I could never remember my left from my right. The first time I had ever left the country I was with Rex. He introduced me to the Garbage Plate at Nick Tahoe's in Rochester, NY. Everything I know about the connection between beer and the history of physics I learned from him, even though a lot of it was probably made up. I spent hours on his "one hour" take-home exams. There is a picture of me, my classmates, and Rex with our middle fingers raised high somewhere out there. Now he's "demonstrating the right hand rule" to St. Peter, hopefully with all the good German beer he could ever want. The world lost a great physics professor and a great person this past year, and I lost a friend and mentor. I hope I manage to become half the professor he was. This book is dedicated to Rex's memory, and in a way, he's indirectly responsible for it being written. If it sucks, then we can blame him!

This is my second book. Writing the first book was such a painful and time-consuming process that I'm absolutely amazed that I agreed to write another. I should thank my family for sticking with me once again, but I think it more appropriate to apologize. My wife Kelly and children Balin and Rory had to put up with my absence for extended periods of time. As I sit here writing this acknowledgement, I'm realizing that I'm about to miss my second Father's Day in a row. Yay deadlines! They never stopped loving me for some reason, and for that I am grateful. My children's love of science but absolute hatred of formal schooling was certainly a motivator to eventually get my books into the hands of practicing teachers. Thankfully, the acknowledgements section is always the last to be written, so I'll soon be seeing a lot more of them, so long as my editor doesn't suck me into writing a third book anytime soon.

Speaking of editors, my editor at Routledge, Lauren Davis, has been extremely patient with me. During the writing of this book I moved half way across the country, started a new job, settled my family into a new city, and almost got involved in a lawsuit. Her patience these past few months as I've pushed back deadline after deadline has been phenomenal. Books are never really finished, only abandoned. That you're reading this indicates that Lauren finally got me to abandon this one. Her work and the work of everyone at Routledge Eye on Education has provided the critical infrastructure and support I've needed to get this thing written and in your hands. You can blame them, too.

Like my previous book *Creating Scientists*, this book is the result of directly working with elementary, middle, and high school science teachers for the past 15 years. It started with a series of workshops on inquiry-based methods in physical science for teachers in Virginia's Prince Edward County Public Schools. These workshops were the brainchild of Laura Williamson, the recently retired director of curriculum and instruction for the district, and funded by Virginia Dominion Power. In South Carolina, my colleague, Louis Rubbo, and I thought that it would be a good idea to design a physics course specifically for pre-service elementary and middle school teachers that addressed standards and used inquiry-based methods to teach practice and thinking. The Division on Undergraduate Education at the National Science Foundation (NSF) gave us a ridiculous amount of your tax dollars for this purpose (NSF-DUE #1244801), with the result being a lot of what you're about to read. Louis and I also learned a lot about developing science thinking working directly with middle school children during summer robotics camps we designed and implemented with computer scientist Brian Larkins, currently at Rhodes College in Memphis. These workshops, the research on science thinking that was built into them, and the work on standards-based hybrid curriculum development discussed in this book was funded by the South Carolina Space Grant Consortium and the II-VI Foundation. I now work in the Omaha, Nebraska metropolitan area, where my job is to build programs that support the area's physical science teachers. The money necessary to do this, as well as a big part of my salary, comes from an endowment funded by Dr. George F. Haddix. My family is particularly thankful for the salary part. This book is based on a graduate course for in-service teachers I began developing at Charles University in Prague, Czech Republic while a Fulbright Scholar. The course and major components of this book have been redeveloped for the University of Nebraska Omaha (UNO) as part of a new graduate program in physics education, with funding coming from the Office of General Education and Dual Enrollment, the College of Arts and Sciences, and the Physics Department.

I have written most of this book sitting in the Kaneko-UNO Library in the Old Market of Omaha, NE. The library is focused on the stimulation and growth of creativity and is a unique partnership between the UNO library and the Kaneko Art Gallery. Every now and then I'll take a break and read a book on street art, pick up something interesting by Steven Pinker, or just wander the gallery. I believe it's improved my productivity and creativity while being a healthier alternative to my previous combination of home office and Scotch, or my office on campus where people can find me and ask me to do stuff. Thank you, UNO library staff and Jun Kaneko, for the great art and awesome facility. This book would probably be slightly more boring without them.

I like to point out that the stuff in my books is based on the work of people that are way smarter than me and that know way more about this stuff than I do. I'm more of a science education research evangelist, preaching the good news handed down by more competent theologians (to stretch the metaphor). The people responsible for the real work are too numerous to list here by name, but if you go through the reference section at the end of each chapter, you'll find them. I read their books and papers and did my best to condense it and make sense of it all, hopefully to save you some time. I will point out that a large part of the specific activities and much of my own thinking about curriculum was heavily influenced by and/or directly adapted from the University of Washington Physics Education Research Group's *Physics by Inquiry*, and the Rutgers University Physics Education Research Group's Investigating Science Learning Environment (ISLE). Without these foundations already existing, there would have been no structure on which to build deep science thinking. Keep in mind, though, that if something in this book sounds stupid or is just plain wrong, it's almost certainly my fault and not theirs.

Finally, I want to acknowledge you for picking up this book and reading it. Science thinking is an absolutely critical component of teaching and learning science. But, it's not really all that glamorous. It's more fun to read whiz-bang books with BuzzFeed-worthy titles like "10 Simple Tricks That Will Get Your Students Smart," usually packed with a handful of neat looking activities and a little substance on how to use them in the classroom. I go a little deeper into the theory in my books, and with science thinking we really have to. It's become clear, and the research we'll get into bears this out, that students don't learn good thinking without some serious support structures. Those support structures are not terribly glamorous to read about. However, you take your job as builder of the next generation seriously. I have a great respect for that, and I hope the information in this book makes that job a little easier. Thank you.

Introduction: Cooks versus Chefs. Knowing versus Understanding

"A home cook who relies too much on a recipe is sort of like a pilot who reads the plane's instruction manual while flying. . . . It's a process that you can't do if you're so completely focused on a recipe."

—Alton Brown (Benn, 2011)

For the past 15 years I've been training myself to cook. As I've gotten better, I've learned that being a good cook goes well beyond knowing how to read and follow a recipe. Following recipes is a good place to start, but there are certain skills you have to learn to get some things right. The advent of the internet has significantly helped my cooking game, because now I can watch Gordon Ramsey or Alton Brown expertly dice an onion and then practice myself. This combination of read-observe-practice has improved my kitchen skills and has resulted in better results as I work through recipes. I'm starting to be a pretty good cook.

The more I progress in the kitchen, though, the more I realize that there is a distinct difference between a good home cook, which I have started to become, and a good home chef, which I want to work towards becoming. The combination of kitchen skills and expertly-designed recipes results in some pretty great food, and my wife and kids are certainly happy that I've chosen this as my hobby. However, to be a decent home chef I need more than a book of recipes and some skills. I need to combine the content knowledge, practices, and reasoning processes of the chef to start innovating in the kitchen. In a sense, I'm going to have to "start over," making horrible dishes as I learn to combine ingredients in different ways, processing the feedback from those dishes, and learning from that feedback. I'm going to have to learn how to *create* food as opposed to just preparing food.

The following is a quote attributed to the great "philosopher" Homer Simpson, which I have come across in internet memes with unknown origins, where Homer is looking in the refrigerator and hungry. I use it here because it aptly describes the separation between the cook and the chef:

There is no food. Just ingredients to make food.

The cook opens the refrigerator looking for the items on their recipe's list. The chef opens the refrigerator and creates recipes based on what's there. Being a chef, as opposed to a cook, requires a certain type of creativity, where knowledge of food is combined with practices and skills to make something unique to the moment and ingredients on hand. Where does that creativity come from? How do we learn it? Can we? How would we teach it?

For me to become a home chef, there is a massive amount of content knowledge to be learned, such as what different ingredients taste like, smoke points of different oils, and even some really cool food science content such as how collagen molecules contract or relax at various temperatures. Specific skills need to be mastered, such as sautéing, braising, chopping the onion I mentioned above, and even sharpening knives. I need to practice like the chef, which means I need to experiment with new flavor combinations and textures, and I need to accept that the practice of cooking can lead to some bad results from time to time, from which I can learn and grow. Finally, to become a decent home chef, I need to understand how the practices of the chef connect to the flavors – what's the reasoning that connects the doing with the knowing? What type of thinking does it take to connect knowledge about triglyceride melting points to the practice of preparing a moist and tender brisket and how might

I generalize this knowledge to figure out how to make this pork shoulder? That right there is the creativity: *thinking*.

You may be slightly confused by now. Isn't this a book about teaching *science* thinking? Why this detailed discussion about food? Are you just trying to make me hungry? How does thinking like a chef fit in with a book about thinking like a scientist?

I'm highlighting the process it takes to become a home chef because it's relatable and is the exact same process required to become a young scientist. In my previous book *Creating Scientists*, I went into depth about what it takes to teach children science as a process, as opposed to a manual full of stuff to know (Moore, 2017). Is it our job to just teach "science facts?" Can we create great biologists by forcing students to memorize the parts of the cell? If the physical science student learns enough equations, are they then prepared to solve new challenges and make new discoveries? Is a chemist born the moment they've learned all of the elements on the periodic table? Are flash cards and memory tasks really a good way to excite the next generation about the practice of science?

It turns out that we can't teach an aspiring chef how to make delicious food by merely having them recite the five basic tastes. Similarly, we can't teach an aspiring scientist how to discover by having them memorize the periodic table of the elements. Sure, that content knowledge *is* a necessary component, but it isn't sufficient for chef or scientist making. If we keep peeling the layers of the onion (ha!), we'll find that it goes deeper than that, as well. Having good knife skills doesn't make a great chef. Having excellent mathematical ability doesn't make a great physicist or even a great mathematician. Skills and abilities *are* necessary, but once again they aren't sufficient.

How can you understand cooking that goes beyond learning to follow a recipe or chopping onions? How can you understand science that goes beyond learning scientific facts or manipulating equations? Ultimately, it requires three things: *knowing*, *doing*, and *thinking*. It takes the synthesis of these three things to be a practicing chef or scientist. My first book *Creating Scientists* focused heavily on knowing and doing, or the content knowledge and practices required of the scientist. This book focuses on the thinking.

Thinking is the glue that binds knowing and doing. Thinking is the creativity required to discover, whether we're talking about discovering new flavor combinations or what happens past the event horizon of a black hole. This is a book about teaching your students how to think, and therefore how to combine knowledge and practice to create.

Teaching Thinking Is Hard

To get you prepared for what's ahead and hopefully motivate you, I'm going to share with you my story. This story is about how I learned to transform my own classroom into a place for deep science thinking.

A long time ago I decided that I wanted to teach science thinking to elementary and middle school pre-service teachers. I had just become a young assistant professor of physics at Longwood University, which is one of the largest producers of teachers in the Commonwealth of Virginia. As the new guy with no power, I was assigned to teach the course every physics professor hates: the general education physical science course filled with not-physics-majors. A massive percentage of the students in my classes were future teachers.

As a former secondary science teacher myself, I was actually excited to take on this population. I approached my department chair and asked her if I could design and teach a different type of physical science course specifically for this population of future teachers based on a new curriculum called *Physics by Inquiry* developed at the University of Washington (McDermott, 1996). She agreed.

I was excited about this new course, because every single day in class we would be doing experiments. There wasn't a single minute of lecture, so students would have to learn science by doing science. The intention was to provide our pre-service teachers with a physical science experience that was more like what we wanted them to do in their future classrooms. This excitement continued during the first offering because the course was actually a lot of fun for me, and the feedback from my students was very positive. It turns out playing is more fun than listening to lectures, even for college-aged adults.

At this time, the Next Generation Science Standards[1] (NGSS) had not yet been written. However, this course revolved around the use of science practices to discover science content. I like to say I was doing three-dimensional teaching before it was cool.

To see if the course was "working," I ran several different research-verified assessments. We tested students' understanding of content in several areas before and after the course, and it turns out that this curriculum worked exceedingly well at teaching content. This was to be expected since the curriculum had been designed and thoroughly tested by one of the teams that invented the field of physics education research.

What hadn't been determined yet was whether or not this curriculum led to gains in students' science thinking abilities. True understanding requires the integration of knowing, doing, and thinking, so do they get any better at the latter? I tested for these abilities, too, since I was certain that a radically constructivist course with constant doing and thinking in science would lead to massive improvements. I was very, very wrong. I found absolutely *zero* improvements in science thinking. None. Not even a little, tiny, itsy-bitsy gain in science thinking ability. Students learned and retained more content than I ever thought possible, but their science thinking abilities stayed absolutely static (Rubbo & Moore, 2012).

It turns out that I wasn't alone. The research on the teaching and learning of science thinking is absolutely clear, and over the past decade it has become even clearer: teaching thinking is really, really hard. So hard, in fact, that a four-year college education *in a science discipline* would result in absolutely *zero* improvement in science thinking (Ding, et al., 2016). This depressing scene didn't change much when we looked at primary and secondary education. In most situations, children either "got" science, or they didn't. And if they didn't, then they never would. The result was the same whether you used older, more traditional approaches to teaching or radically reformed inquiry-based methods.

I wasn't willing to give up, and thankfully my colleagues in this field didn't give up either. Over the next decade I integrated what we knew about teaching thinking into my work with future teachers, and in the process I'd discovered a few things myself. Our understanding of cognition and educational psychology has dramatically improved over the past decade, and there is more and more evidence piling up showing that science thinking can be taught. I personally know that it can because I have data from my own classes that show significant gains in science thinking when implementing the ideas discussed in this book (Moore, 2017).

You can teach and students can learn science thinking. We can teach them how to create using their minds. However, it's definitely not easy. In comparison, it's really easy to teach content. It's a little harder to teach science practice compared to content, but significantly easier to teach compared to thinking. Blending all three in your instruction, knowing, doing, and thinking, is harder still, and necessary. Teaching science thinking takes dedication to the task, and learning thinking requires significant support structures.

This book is a compendium of proven support structures for teaching science thinking that I hope helps you in your efforts to make children more awesome.

The Next Generation Science Standards, Thinking, and Crosscutting Concepts

If it's so hard, why would you want to teach science thinking? The National Research Council's excellent document *A Framework for K-12 Science Education* (which I'll refer to as simply the *Framework* throughout the rest of the book) describes a future for science education that is based on the "three-dimensional" view of understanding I've described (National Research Council, 2012). Specifically, the *Framework* specifies an approach to teaching and learning in science that blends doing science and thinking scientifically in order to know science content. The NGSS are based on the *Framework*, and the explicit performance expectations built into these new standards clearly expect students to demonstrate abilities in knowing, doing, and thinking (NGSS Lead States, 2013a).

Basically, if your state has adopted the NGSS or standards like them, then you don't get to want to teach science thinking. You have to!

In my previous book *Creating Scientists*, we went into great depth about what the NGSS calls disciplinary core ideas (DCIs) and science practices. However, in that book I didn't go into great depth about the third leg of the three-legged stool: science thinking. If you read the book, thinking was discussed and incorporated into the activities described throughout. (If you haven't read the book, then you should!) However, the concepts of science practice and science thinking are each so big and so new to the busy teacher that my publisher and I decided to focus on each in separate books. So, *Creating Scientists* focused on the practices and their relation to the DCIs in the NGSS, while this book will focus on the thinking, or what is woven deep into the fabric of what the NGSS calls "crosscutting concepts."

A lot of what the NGSS and *Framework* describe as "crosscutting concepts" are actually science reasoning patterns used by all types of scientists. Let's take a look at the NGSS crosscutting concepts and think about how they relate to science thinking. The seven crosscutting concepts are as follows (NGSS Lead States, 2013b):

1. Patterns
2. Cause and effect
3. Scale, proportion, and quantity
4. Systems and system models
5. Energy and matter
6. Structure and function
7. Stability and change.

As we progress through the book, we'll talk about all of these crosscutting concepts in more detail. Specifically, we'll discuss how most of these seven concepts are really just scientific reasoning patterns used by scientists across all fields.

For one example to introduce you to this idea, let's look at patterns and think about a young child learning that a glowing red burner on a stove is hot. Simply telling the child that the stove is hot doesn't mean that they understand the concept of "hot" and "burn." Unfortunately, a good observation experiment (we'll talk about these more later) may be needed, where the child begins to learn about hotness by touching the stove and experiencing the resulting pain. Ideally, they just get their hand close enough to feel the heat and that is sufficient.

Here, the child is combining the science practices of asking questions, performing investigations, and analyzing data to come up with some new science content: glowing red burners on stoves are hot, and that means they can burn me! But let's go further. As the child grows, they naturally experience more and more. At some point, they "discover" that glowing red charcoal is also hot and burns when touched. Glowing lightbulbs are hot and burn. The sun glows, and it sure is hot out when the sun is beating down on them. The young mind begins to recognize a pattern: glowing things are usually hot things. This pattern recognition is a science thinking ability. It links the science doing with the science knowing, and the child now has a true understanding of the connection between "glowing" and "hot."

We'll look at the other crosscutting concepts and how some of them are fundamentally science thinking as we move through the book. We'll also explore more useful classroom activities than the one I just described (please, please, please don't teach your class about heat by shoving their hands on hot stove burners!) For now, though, you should have a good introduction to the idea of science thinking, how it connects to knowing and doing, why it's important, and how it's integrated into new science standards.

What Does This Mean for You, the Busy Teacher?

What does this new paradigm and fancy new way of teaching and learning mean for you, besides more work? It is probably an understatement to say that teachers are not big fans of implementing big changes in standards. The tough, in-the-trenches work falls squarely on your shoulders. The NGSS does represent a fundamentally new paradigm for teaching and assessing science, and teaching young children how to think about abstract and multi-faceted ideas is certainly not easy. Assessing content knowledge is hard enough. In *Creating Scientists*, we looked at how to assess practices, and in those cases we at least had visible actions and exemplars to examine. How in the world will you, the teacher, get into the mind of your students to assess their *thinking*!

To get you ready, the NGSS writing teams identified several "conceptual shifts" that you, the science educator will need to make to effectively use the new standards (NGSS Lead States, 2013c). For the purposes of this book, I want to highlight three of these conceptual shifts. The shifts are as follows:

1. K–12 science education should reflect the real-world interconnections in science.
2. Science concepts build coherently across K–12.
3. The NGSS focus on deeper understanding and application of content.

Science education should reflect the real-world interconnections in science. Those interconnections many times manifest in content, but where the sciences are *really* connected are with respect to the practices of scientists and their thinking processes. Biology, chemistry, physics, and earth science are now expected to highlight these crosscutting practices and reasoning abilities, and make sure our students know that the types of abilities they are learning in biology class directly carry over to chemistry class. At the elementary level, this is easier in principle, because typically the same teacher is covering all of those disciplines. However, as the teaching of science breaks off into separate courses, it can be more complicated to coordinate across disciplines. The NGSS makes sure we all focus on the same crosscutting concepts from classroom to classroom.

Another conceptual shift you will need to make in your teaching is that science concepts build coherently across K-12. As you will see, the science thinking you are expected to teach and assess are *the same across all age groups*. As a former high school physical science teacher, I know too well that it is easy to build walls around our little domains. We often fail to realize what students are even learning in middle school, much less elementary school. It was hard enough for me to get a handle on the state-based standards in my little area, much less other age group's standards. With the NGSS, we are all playing on the same team, working with the same set of practices and crosscutting concepts that we are being asked to teach and assess. Ideally, this provides the student with a unified and coherent picture of what science is and how it is done that is consistent as they move up the grade levels, even though the sophistication may increase.

Finally, you are expected to teach towards a deeper understanding and application of content. What does "deeper understanding" really mean? It means that we want students to really learn content through the application of science practices and thinking in an authentic manner. We want students to discover content authentically, so that they understand not only the content, but how science practice leads us to knowledge and how science thinking allows us to know that the knowledge is true. Once again: *knowing*, *doing*, and *thinking*.

Unfortunately, what this all really means for you the practicing teacher is possibly a very dramatic rethinking of what you are doing in your classroom and the assessments you are using to evaluate your students' learning. I will not sugar coat it: the NGSS means more work for you. I hope the following chapters will help to lessen that burden.

What Will You Learn from This Book?

In the following chapters, I will provide:

1. an approachable introduction to the relevant research on what science thinking is, how it can be taught, and how it can be assessed, (something traditional science pedagogy does not achieve);
2. specific, immediately deployable classroom activities, including generic "Thinking Task" worksheets that can be incorporated into existing lessons; and

3. a framework you can use to integrate science thinking into your lessons for your specific content needs – all in the context of next generation standards worldwide, like the Core and NGSS in the United States.

The framework and activities described in the book are research-verified, and will provide you the classroom tools necessary to help your students obtain the following thinking strategies:

◆ Recognizing patterns, learning, and practicing how a scientist thinks up a hypothesis.
◆ Correlations and causation: did this thing over here cause that action over there?
◆ What's important in an experiment, what's not, and designing a fair test.
◆ Testing our crazy ideas with experiments that provide support or falsification.
◆ What does this evidence tell me, and do I believe it?
◆ Comparing proportions and scales, and thinking about really big (or small) things.

Every bit of that list is built into the NGSS crosscutting concepts, plus a little bit more. In *Creating Scientists* we asked the following questions: how do you teach a student to plan and carry out their own investigation? More importantly, how would you possibly assess something like that? In this book, we wonder how we go even further and teach the student how to evaluate the relative value of the evidence their experiment produces. What patterns emerge in the data? Can we connect our content knowledge with this new data to form a hypothesis? Can we then test that hypothesis? Basically, we're going to discuss how to teach the student to think, and then we're going to try to assess that thinking. Hopefully, once you've finished this book you will have the necessary tools.

Specifically, this book has the following learning outcomes for you the reader:

After reading this book, you will be able to:

1. use a research-verified framework of generative principles to create and/or adapt your own lessons that improve the science thinking of your students;

2. assess your students' learning within these domains for the NGSS crosscutting concepts or any standards framework with focus on the integration of science thinking with practice and content; and

3. link your approach to teaching to well established research in science education.

You will be able to track your personal growth and progress relative to these outcomes through the formative assessment methods described in the book. For those of you that are in-service teachers, the incorporation of immediately deployable, and research-verified classroom activities will allow you to begin implementation with known, effective materials. As you begin to use the framework to create new lessons, the growth in your teaching abilities will be trackable through assessment of your students' learning.

The book itself takes a *model-mentor-monitor* approach that mirrors the process of "cognitive apprenticeship" I am promoting throughout the book. Special features of this book include the following:

◆ Sample classroom activities – concrete models of how to do the work
◆ Frameworks for creating new activities – how to use the generative principles in the models for new situations
◆ Sample formative and summative assessment rubrics – to monitor progress and inform future teaching moves
◆ Frameworks for creating new assessment rubrics
◆ Complete "Thinking Task" worksheets that can be immediately incorporated into existing lessons to make science thinking explicit, to have your students reflect on science thinking, and to make science thinking count in your students' grades.

Furthermore, the end-of-chapter reference sections will lead you to the relevant literature, theory and research so that you can understand why the activities work and can therefore develop and justify your own instruction using the same principles. My own research in science thinking and practice has shown that an explicit approach to these topics is required, where students are consistently required to think about their own thinking. The exact same approach is required for teachers to learn these abilities and learn how to teach them. Hopefully, you will think deeply about the content in this book by putting the lessons into practice, evaluating their effectiveness, and reassessing your own goals for your students.

An Outline

The first three chapters of the book answer three basic questions:

1. What is science thinking?
2. How is science thinking integrated into next generation standards?
3. How do you teach and assess science thinking?

In Chapter 1, I will describe what is meant by the term "science thinking." Specifically, I will discuss how experts do science, the practices they employ, and the ways they think about science. I will also describe how the student views science, the wide gulf between the student and the expert, and how "traditional" teaching can actually reinforce novice views of science and bad practices. We will review the science education and science philosophy research literature to specifically define a set of generally accepted science thinking patterns. These science thinking patterns will become the foundation we will want to establish in the minds of our K–12 science students.

In Chapter 2, we will see how knowing, doing, and thinking are incorporated into emerging science standards around the world, with a specific focus on the NGSS in the USA. We will look at what the NGSS refers to as crosscutting concepts and identify how these align with the science thinking patterns we identify from the research literature in Chapter 1.

In Chapter 3, I will describe the framework you can use to teach and assess science thinking. In particular, I will discuss classroom-based *cognitive apprenticeship* as a framework you can use to teach science thinking to your students. You will learn how to create *authentic science experiences* in the classroom, where students engage in authentic science practice, work together to build truth from evidence, and reflect on those truths and the processes they used in their acquisition – combining knowing, doing, and thinking. I will also discuss the importance of being very explicit in your activities about what the students are doing and why they are doing it, having the students reflect on their thinking, and making science thinking "count" when grading.

Chapters 4–7 go through research-verified examples of classroom lessons that are based on the NGSS and are built from the framework described in the preceding chapters. You will see how we designed and deployed the lessons, examples of actual student work, how that work was assessed, and practical tips on how you can use the lessons in your classroom. Each chapter focuses on one or two of the science thinking patterns outlined in Chapter 1. In each chapter, I will provide simple "Thinking Task" worksheets that you can use to begin the conversation about science thinking with your students.

The example content in this book focuses on physical science throughout the grade levels. (I have degrees in physics and chemistry, after all.) However, it is important to point out that the science practices themselves are crosscutting, and by definition the crosscutting concepts (the thinking) are also . . . crosscutting! It's right there in the name. Content is just the context in which the lessons are done. You'll learn useful tips no matter what subject you teach.

And finally, Chapter 8 describes how you can put all the pieces together. I'll go through the entire curriculum development process, built for one NGSS performance expectation on magnetic fields in middle school physical science. We'll use the lessons learned throughout the book and the generative curriculum development process discussed in Chapter 3 to build an entire learning sequence. We will discuss how we defined learning goals, weaved thinking into the sequence, built the learning experiences, and what we looked for in student work as markers for success. Finally, I'll also show you how to incorporate experiments into summative assessments and tease out student reasoning to determine what's going on in their minds.

Let's Create Great Chefs Instead of Just Good Cooks

Some people think great chefs are born. However, any good chef will tell you that it takes thousands of hours of training, practice, and honing of the craft to come anywhere close to being considered "good." Great chefs aren't born, they're created through hard work and good teaching. Scientists are similar. I have never met an infant that could solve humanity's problems. I have met scientists that can, and those scientists worked hard over years to learn the abilities needed. Every great scientist has learned to integrate *knowing, doing,* and *thinking,* whether or not they knew that's what they were doing. Everyone has to learn to be a chef or a scientist, and therefore they must be taught. I want your help teaching the next generation.

To remind you, teaching thinking is exceptionally hard. I want you sufficiently warned that when you focus on thinking in your classroom, there will be struggle. However, the struggle will ultimately pay off in the end. We don't need every student to ultimately become a scientist, or even most of them. We don't need everyone to be a chef. We do need a well-prepared citizenry, though, that can think critically about all types of topics. So even though everyone doesn't need to leave secondary school to pursue a culinary or physics degree, we still want a population that can think like chefs and scientists instead of just cooks and encyclopedias.

Let's create some great science thinkers together!

Note

1 Next Generation Science Standards is a registered trademark of Achieve. Neither Achieve nor the lead states and partners that developed the Next Generation Science Standards were involved in the production of this product, and do not endorse it.

References

Benn, E. (2011, October 4). Alton Brown says improvising is key in the kitchen. *St. Louis Post-Dispatch*.

Ding, L., Wei, X., & Mollohan, K. (2016). Does Higher Education Improve Student Scientific Reasoning Skills? *International Journal of Science and Mathematics Education, 14*(4), 619–634.

McDermott, L. C. (1996). *Physics by Inquiry*. New York: John Wiley & Sons.

Moore, C. (2017). *Creating Scientists: Teaching and Assessing Science Practice for the NGSS*. New York, NY: Routledge.

National Research Council. (2012). *A Framework for K-12 Science Education: Practices, Crosscutting Concepts, and Core Ideas*. Washington, DC: The National Academies Press.

NGSS Lead States. (2013). *The Next Generation Science Standards: For States, By States*. Washington, DC: The National Academies Press.

Rubbo, L., & Moore, J. (2012). Are We Teaching Students to Think Like Scientists? *Connecting People to Science: A National Conference on Science Education and Public Outreach, 457*, 343–347.

Part I
Teaching and Learning Science Thinking

1

What Is Science Thinking?

"Is scientific thinking of any relevance outside of science? I answer this question with an emphatic yes and portray scientific thinking as a human activity engaged in by most people, rather than a rarefied few."

—Deanna Kuhn (Kuhn, 2004, p. 2)

If we want to teach students how to think like scientists, then we first have to define science thinking. Sociologists have spent decades following natural and physical scientists around and observing their behavior in an effort to answer two important questions:

1. What do scientists do? and
2. How do scientists think?

According to these sociologists, "science thinking" can be fundamentally defined as the way expert scientists think about problems in their field – "science thinking" is the thinking done by scientists (Latour, 1987). There are a few other ways to think about science thinking. However, if we can teach students to think and act like practicing scientists, then in the process they will learn the community accepted practices for discovering new truths about the physical world around them, and the important critical thinking abilities necessary to know that what they are doing is scientific.

It all seems simple enough, but it still presents us with the question: how exactly does a scientist think? When a scientist is confronted with a specific problem, what processes go on in their mind? When staring at data, what thoughts do they have? How does an expert scientist think about science, and how does a novice student think about science? The focus of this chapter is on answering these questions.

First, we're going to have to define what we mean by the word "understanding," because that's what we ultimately want our students to do: understand science. We'll discuss the cognitive science behind the *Framework*'s and the NGSS's view of understanding and how science thinking is fundamentally integrated into that view. We'll dig a little deeper into the brief discussion we had in the introduction and detail the three-legged stool that props up understanding: *knowing, doing,* and *thinking.*

Then, we'll look at students' views about science and their fundamental epistemologies when it comes to learning science. This is a fancy way of saying that we'll examine what the student *thinks they should be thinking.* Then, we'll look at how scientists view the learning of science, or what the student *should be thinking.* As an educated science teacher, you will probably not be surprised by how the professional scientist thinks about science; however, you may be surprised by how students think about science, its practices, and what they think is important to the learning of science. We will examine the typical student's view of what science is and compare that to the expert's view, exposing the wide gap between the two. This will be important when we start to look at how to teach thinking throughout the rest of the book. If we aren't careful, the laboratories and many classroom activities we use could actually *reinforce* the student's novice view of science, and lead to the propagation of poor thinking.

As we continue this chapter, we'll look at the research literature on scientific thinking, how it's informed by scientists' views about the nature of science, and I'll do my best to define it as clearly as possible in a way that is useful for the classroom. In this context, I'll review the more authentic scientific method I have discussed in my previous book *Creating Scientists.* If you haven't read that book (you should!), then you'll discover the more authentic, and therefore more messy, process by which scientists actually perform science. It's not necessarily the linear, hypothesis-driven process found in the first chapter of most science textbooks. We'll see how the thinking patterns of the expert scientist weave into the science process and discuss what philosophers of science believe science thinking is.

This chapter deals primarily with defining science thinking and seeing how it integrates with practice. I'm trying to keep this chapter as universal as possible, and I won't focus on any specific standards. In the next chapter, we'll look at how science thinking is integrated into new science standards in the USA, and what's expected students should be able to do with respect to science thinking throughout their K–12 education.

Understanding Requires Knowing, Doing, and Thinking

We want our students to *understand* science, so we need to start with a theoretical model for how we as humans come to understand anything. *Situated cognition* is a learning theory that assumes understanding to be situated in actions that occur within cultural, social, and physical contexts. In simpler language, knowledge is inseparable from doing. More importantly, knowledge cannot be separated from the means in which the knowledge is learned by the community that "knows" it (Brown, Collins, & Duguid, 1989). In our case, situated cognition tells us that students can only understand science or humanities or any types of ideas if they understand how the practice and thinking of the practitioner leads to those ideas.

This will be the framework on which the ideas in this book will be built. It's very important, because it's also the foundation of what we call *Three-Dimensional Teaching and Learning*, as outlined in the *Framework* and the NGSS (National Research Council, 2012; NGSS Lead States, 2013a).

What does it mean "to understand" a topic? Figure 1.1 shows a simple cartoon that really highlights the main point I'm trying to get across in this book. We will revisit this figure throughout the book, because it encapsulates the main point of next generation teaching in the sciences.

Figure 1.1 Understanding requires the synthesis of knowing, doing, and thinking

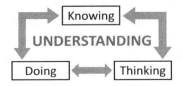

If you finish reading this book, and all that you have managed to absorb and remember is this figure, then I will have accomplished my goal.

Within the framework we will use (and on which the NGSS is built), three fundamental components combine within the learner's mind to form a deep understanding: 1. *knowing*, 2. *doing*, and 3. *thinking*. To understand, the learner needs sufficient content knowledge, the practice abilities necessary to discover or know that the content knowledge is true, and the appropriate reasoning to link the practice to the knowledge. These three components can be considered the three legs of a three-legged stool: remove one leg, and the stool falls down. Similarly, the absence of either component within some context results in a lack of true understanding of that context. The learner may know facts, but without the underlying context of how those facts came to be known, and the thinking required to link actions to knowing, the learner does not understand the content that they know.

For example, let's revisit the example we discussed in the introduction of the hot stove and the small child. If we tell a small child that the stove is hot and will burn her, does that child now understand the concepts of heat and burning? They might not touch the stove because they were told not to, but they have not truly developed an understanding without also learning how the knowledge that "stove equals danger" came into being. In this instance, we have separated the knowledge from the process of gaining the knowledge.

Similarly, in the context of science, we can tell the student that the mitochondria is the battery of the cell. The student can then repeat this on an examination and label it properly on a diagram. However, does that student now truly understand what the mitochondria is and what it does? I want to highlight that this model of understanding isn't limited to the sciences. For example, the student of literature may be taught and therefore know that the green light in F. Scott Fitzgerald's *The Great Gatsby* is a symbol for the "American dream" broadly, and the character Gatsby's hopes and dreams for the future specifically. However, does the student necessarily understand literary symbols and their construction, identification, and interpretation?

Situated cognition tells us that true understanding does not happen without action. How can the learner find out what the mitochondria does? What evidence can they draw on? Specifically, what actions does the expert scientist perform that lead to knowledge about the mitochondria? How does the learner interpret literary symbols? Can they do so in a new context unaided? What actions does the expert in literature perform that lead to appropriate identification and interpretation? Fundamentally, situated cognition tells us that understanding is a verb, not a noun, as opposed to theories of knowledge as accumulated stuff in our brains.

Understanding takes knowing, doing, and thinking. Understanding within a specific field takes knowing, doing, and thinking in the context of the community that defines the context. In our case, understanding of science requires the student to know science content as specified by the scientific community, do science like scientists in the scientific community, and think like scientists in the scientific community.

Ultimately, how the community of scientists knows, does, and thinks defines for us scientific understanding. Therefore, if we want to define scientific thinking, then we simply have to examine how scientists reason in the performance of their craft. The thinking patterns of the scientist become our goal, with the thinking patterns of the student serving as our starting point.

How Do Students View the Learning of Science?

My own research and that of my colleagues over the past decade has shown that fundamentally, the major distinction between the novice student and the expert scientist is in the way they think about and view science and its practice (Moore, 2012). In particular, the psychology and education professor Deanna Kuhn suggests that the distinction is most clear through their "epistemological appreciation" of how new knowledge is formed (Kuhn, 2004). Epistemology is the study of the nature of knowledge and how we go about acquiring knowledge. This is very relevant to our discussion about science thinking, because it turns out that how a student views the practice of science is fundamentally a function of their epistemological beliefs (Edmondson & Novak, 1993).

As one example, the novice student will often make subconscious justifications for the way they practice and think about science based on their view that science knowledge is "propagated stuff." They use a specific equation to solve some problem because an expert told them that that is how it should be done. Or, they learn that the mitochondria is the "powerhouse of the cell" from their textbook or class lecture. Maybe they memorize the periodic table of the elements for recall on an exam in the future. All of this is science knowledge, but it isn't sense-making, in that they may know the fact but not necessarily the why and how. Their view of knowledge acquisition in the sciences, their epistemology, is that "experts" provide "facts."

If the student gets stuck in this mental framing in the science class, and it seems that they often do, then that student starts seeing science as merely a collection of facts, and experiments as mere ancillaries to learning those facts (Tsai, 1998). Obviously, we want to move students away from this naive view about science, experiments, and the nature of knowledge formation, because this just isn't how science is practiced and it's not how scientists think. If we want students to think like scientists, then we need students to start viewing science as the process that it is.

We can actually learn a lot about how students view science from prior research. For example, the *Views About Sciences Survey* (VASS) is a relatively short and simple pencil-and-paper assessment that probes student and expert views about science along six dimensions (Hestenes & Halloun, 1996). Over the past few decades, this assessment has been deployed in numerous science classrooms around the world. Furthermore, the same assessment has been given to hundreds of professional scientists and science educators. From the results, we can build a fairly good picture of how the novice student views science across these dimensions and compare their views to those of the experts. These novice-like and expert-like views are summarized in Table 1.1 (Hestenes & Halloun, 1998).

TABLE 1.1 TAXONOMY OF STUDENT AND SCIENTIST VIEWS ABOUT SCIENCE

Dimension	How students view science	How scientists view science
Structure	Science is a loose collection of directly perceived facts.	Science is a coherent body of knowledge about patterns in nature.
Methodology	The methods of science are specific to the discipline.	The methods of science are crosscutting.
Validity	Scientific knowledge is exact, absolute, and final.	Scientific knowledge is tentative and refutable.
Learnability	Science is learnable by a few talented people.	Learnable by anyone.
Reflective thinking	For meaningful understanding of science, one needs to memorize facts.	Science is a process that allows for the recognition of patterns.
Personal relevance	Science is of exclusive concern to scientists.	Benefits everyone.

Source: Adapted from Hestenes & Halloun, 1998

For the purposes of this book, let's look at the distinct difference between the student and scientist across the dimensions of structure, methodology, validity, and reflective thinking. These four dimensions make up the foundational views used by students to construct an understanding of the practice of science and how to go about learning and understanding science content. Specifically, results from the VASS suggest that students typically view the structure of science as being a collection of facts, the practice of science as situationally dependent, and the validity of science as being absolute, with no room for growth. Also note that students have an interesting view about how science is learned: *by memorizing facts.*

In contrast, the expert scientist recognizes the tentative nature of science that is an ever-expanding body of knowledge with crosscutting methodologies. The scientist believes the learning of science happens through the practice of science, and that science is ultimately centered on the recognition of patterns in nature. Furthermore, the scientists recognize the utility of science and its methods and practices to areas far removed from their specific scientific disciplines.

How does formal education in science affect student views? Unfortunately, studies have shown that as students go through school, their views about science *actually get worse*! Our teaching could be pushing students *away* from expert-like views about science (Adams, et al., 2006; Shan, 2013). How is this so? Let's look at a few examples of what seems like inquiry-based teaching reinforcing novice-like views. The middle school student might melt ice in a cup and measure the change in temperature as a function of the mass of the ice to demonstrate the already taught "law" that heat transfer is proportional to the mass. The high school student might use this same data to determine the heat capacity of the material. The student may drop items of varying weight from the bleachers to determine that they truly do fall at the same rate. These are examples where the answer is already known. Typically, the experiment is given to the student, too, in a checklist procedure that they blindly follow.

There is not necessarily any real discovery for the student dropping items from the bleachers. It sure is fun, but the student is merely demonstrating a "fact" that they probably already "learned" in class. The hypothesis was set for them from the beginning, and the task itself dictated. The activity may do a great job of reinforcing the learning of content knowledge, but we can start to see how and why a young student might begin to view all science as stuff to be learned, instead of a process to be practiced, and how what we perceive to be quality, hands-on instruction is really reinforcing that naïve view. Furthermore, in most classes, that same student will then be given a high-stakes test that primarily centers on the content knowledge they've "learned," further highlighting the primacy of knowing over doing and thinking in the student's mind.

What are we doing when we spend a majority of our time focusing on the teaching of facts and assessment of the retention of facts? We are reinforcing this novice-like conception about science that it is a collection of facts to be learned, when really science is a process that leads to new knowledge. We can't blame the student if they then focus on facts, because they are rightfully preparing themselves for the tests that we give them.

Now, to be clear, I'm not advocating that we abandon dropping stuff off of bleachers. I'm certainly not saying that we should abandon experiments. In fact, the opposite is true. However, we as teachers have to be cognizant about how our students think and use this knowledge to reflect on the types of activities we do and, more importantly, the types of assessments we use.

As we'll learn in later chapters, a hands-on approach to science is an excellent way to get students engaged in learning, and using the practices and thinking we want them to master. It's fun, which makes learning easier, and you can't really learn how to do and think without actually doing and thinking. However, if students view science as facts to learn, and you assess students on their ability to recall facts, then they will rightly conclude that all of that fun hands-on stuff is ancillary as opposed to fundamental. They'll miss the point of science.

What Is Expert-Like Science Thinking?

The big take-away from the VASS is that the fundamental thinking process of the student is memorization, and we'll use this view throughout the book to inform our teaching of good science thinking. The expert, on the other hand, knows that memorization doesn't lead to discovery, so their thinking as they perform science is much more complicated. We know from the VASS how expert scientists view the process of science, but the survey doesn't tell us the specific thinking patterns that they use as they work. Let's now start examining how the scientist thinks while doing science. What's going on in their minds?

What exactly constitutes scientific thinking is complex and surprisingly debatable; however, we can discover some common themes. The science education theorist Anton Lawson has proposed that scientific reasoning and its practice fundamentally has a structure that he describes as being "hypothetical-deductive" in nature (Lawson, 2005). This means scientists make hypotheses and deduce the consequences. This aspect of science thinking is primarily deductive. There are laws from which we deduce results. If the results are shown in reality, then the law is valid, otherwise the law must be revised. Lawson suggests that all of scientific reasoning is chiefly hypothetical-deductive in nature and consists of interrelated aspects, such as proportional reasoning, control of variables, probability reasoning, and correlation reasoning, all of which are used in hypothesis-testing experiments (Lawson, 1982; Lawson, 2005).

There is no doubt that deductive process is at the heart of much of science thinking; however, many practicing scientists, science philosophers, and education theorists and practitioners have concluded that this traditional and ridged view of science thinking is just too simplistic a model of science alone to describe how science is done and the thinking of the scientist. Real, authentic science is much messier and the thinking more complex.

In particular, how do scientists come up with hypotheses in the first place? Science historian and philosopher Douglas Allchin argues that throughout the modern history of science, much of scientific discovery can be described as inductive in nature (Allchin, 2003). What this means is that often scientists have *absolutely no clue* why or how certain phenomena occur, such that hazarding a guess, or hypothesis, would be of little value. Instead, scientists developed useful tools for identifying regularities, patterns, and associations. Instead of blindly identifying a hypothesis to test, observations can be made where patterns in the resulting data are used to devise a hypothesis. Ultimately, inductive and deductive process are involved, with some researchers intimately linking science thinking with the process of drawing inferences from initial premises (Holyoak & Morrison, 2005; Overton, 1990).

More recently, the psychology and education professor Deanna Kuhn has suggested that scientific thinking is more than inductive and deductive inference, but also a truth-seeking social process that involves the coordination of theory and evidence (Kuhn, 2004). Let's unpack that statement, because there are two ideas here: 1. science is a social process, and 2. the thinking involved in connecting evidence to ideas and evaluating the relative value of the evidence is a critical component of science thinking. As we saw in Table 1.1, the scientist believes that science is tentative and refutable. Therefore, there must be some type of thinking process that they use to determine the value of any specific piece of evidence. Furthermore, that thinking is shaped by the entire community of practicing scientists.

From this short and relatively simplistic review of the literature on scientific thinking, we can reduce a complex and debatable topic into seven basic thinking patterns used by scientists on which we can work with our students in the classroom. Table 1.2 details the following seven science thinking patterns:

◆ Pattern recognition
◆ Causation
◆ Determining relevant variables and isolating them
◆ Hypothetical-deductive thinking
◆ Metacognition and the relative value of evidence
◆ Proportional thinking.

Pattern recognition is the foundation of science. Ultimately, science only works because nature keeps repeating itself. The scientist's job is to discover these repeating patterns, observe how they repeat, determine

TABLE 1.2 FOUNDATIONAL SCIENCE THINKING PATTERNS

Thinking pattern	Description
Pattern Recognition	Discover repeating patterns in nature, observe how they repeat, determine why they repeat, and use models of the patterns to make new predictions.
Causative Thinking	Investigating and explaining causes of patterns. Determining how repeating patterns are influenced by relevant factors. Real causative mechanisms can be tested and the cause-effect linking variables ascertained.
Control of Variables	Recognize relevant variables that may influence patterns in nature. Isolate and control these variables in experiments to make tests fair so that useful conclusions can be drawn about how individual variables affect patterns.
Hypothetical-Deductive	Combine hypothesis-generation with control of variables to form a complete reasoning chain connecting a hypothesis to a specific test, result, and judgement. Ultimately, hypothetical-deductive reasoning is the thinking involved in hypothesis-testing.
Metacognition	Evaluate the thinking process itself. This evaluation includes thinking about how the uncertainties in measurements might affect judgements.
Proportional Thinking	Recognize what is relevant at different measures of size, time, and energy. Recognize how changes in the scale, size, or quantity can affect behavior.

why they repeat, and use models of the patterns to make new predictions. Therefore, the student of science needs the thinking abilities to recognize and observe patterns. These patterns can manifest as repeating forms, such as shapes and colors of specific fish species, or repeating events, such as seasons or solar eclipses. Pattern thinking goes beyond simple recognition, though. Good science thinking requires the ability to use patterns to organize and classify content, as well as prompt questions about the relationships and/or variables that might influence the pattern.

These patterns have causes, which can be simple or complex and a function of multiple variables. Part of science thinking is investigating and explaining these causal relationships. Does doing this thing over here *cause* that result over there? Sometimes, we notice repeating patterns that seem influenced by some factor, but that factor might not be the cause. It's correlative but not causative. As an example, you might notice that plastic bottles of soda keep exploding when you leave them in the trunk of your car and conclude that trunks cause soda bottles to explode. Later on, you realize that this only seems to happen when it is hot outside. Was the trunk the cause? Real causative mechanisms can be tested and the cause-effect linking variables ascertained.

To understand how different variables might affect patterns, the scientist must be able to control those variables within their minds as well as in practice as they design experiments to probe the how and why of a pattern. Control of variables has two components:

1. the recognition of relevant variables, and
2. the ability to isolate and control those variables in experiments.

For example, you notice that the plastic bottles of soda in your trunk only seem to expand and explode in your car trunk during hot summer months. You might rightly conclude that the temperature is a relevant variable. Moving forward, you could devise an experiment to explore the relationship. Isolation of variables means that you will try to control other possible influences while only changing the temperature. Maybe you ensure that the types of soda are kept consistent, or that the bottles all have the same shape and size.

Once the scientist has observed and explored some pattern in nature and they discover some causal link between variables, they can begin to start explaining why the pattern happens with the ultimate goal of coming up with some model that they can use to predict future behavior. This type of mental activity is called hypothesis-generation, where the scientist uses their observations to form new hypotheses. The thinking pattern called hypothetical-deductive reasoning combines hypothesis-generation with control of variables to form a complete reasoning chain connecting the hypothesis to a specific test, result, and judgement. Ultimately, hypothetical-deductive reasoning is the thinking involved in hypothesis-testing.

When making judgements, the scientist recognizes that all measurements in science come with some degree of uncertainty. For example, we can measure the length of a string using a ruler and get a pretty good estimate of its length. However, the ruler itself has some limitations, such as the spacing between the markings. The string could also have some elasticity, which means its length could vary slightly with the amount of force being applied to it. We can still learn a lot about the string length, but there is always some uncertainty. Maybe all of the soda bottles don't explode in your trunk at the same time or at all, but most of them do and within a certain timeframe. Good science thinking incorporates this uncertainty in the evaluation of the relative value of evidence. A good scientist can make a judgement using the results of some experiment, but can maintain a sense of skepticism and a variable amount of confidence in their judgement based on the degree to which they know something. Now, keep in mind our discussion earlier: students fundamentally think science is absolute and final, so it will take a lot to get them to think about their own thinking.

Finally, in considering phenomena, the scientist recognizes that some things may be more or less relevant at different measures of size, time, and/or energy. This type of thinking is called proportional thinking. During the short drive home from the grocery store, none of the soda bottles explode. It seems to take a certain amount of time and possibly a certain amount of energy, like forgetting them for days during an extreme heat wave. Those with short drives or who walk to the store may never experience an exploded bottle of soda, because the time and energy considerations are outside any range where such effects would be visible. These bottles are designed *not* to explode in normal circumstances, after all. Furthermore, a change in scale when measuring our little piece of string could seriously affect our assessment of its length. Measure the simple piece of string in units of kilometers, and the right answer to what its length is may be as simple as "really, really small." To the astronaut in space, the string in your hand wouldn't even be a consideration. It's a single point.

Obviously, this is not an exhaustive list of thinking patterns used by professional scientists. Table 1.2 takes everything we've learned from the literature on scientific thinking and condenses it down into a series of thinking patterns that are universal and routinely used by scientists. This is sufficient for our needs, since it is not realistic to believe that high school graduates should be completely prepared for careers as professional scientists. Furthermore, there is some debate among science philosophers and cognitive scientists about the fundamental "nature" of scientific thinking. The intricacies of this debate aren't really for us, either. Our mission is to get our K–12 students set on the right course, and for that we need a framework. The seven thinking patterns listed are an entry point for an informed citizenry that understands not only basic scientific content, but also the methods by which scientific knowledge is obtained, and how scientists think in the process of discovery.

How Do Experts Integrate Thinking into Practice?

You might notice that there is a lot of overlap between the different thinking patterns. Specifically, if you look at Table 1.2, you'll notice that the concept of pattern recognition appears in almost all of the descriptions for the different thinking patterns. We found similar overlap among the various science practices discussed in *Creating Scientists*. Furthermore, the thinking also heavily overlaps the doing. When building a taxonomy of thinking patterns and doing practices of the scientist, it's impossible to not find overlap between the two and between their constituents. This is the nature of science-as-process.

We really can't separate the doing from the thinking if we want to teach three-dimensionally. So, let's see how these science thinking patterns are incorporated into science doing.

As I described in my previous book *Creating Scientists*, the typical science textbook will usually start with a description of the "scientific method," generally with an illustration similar to that shown in Figure 1.2. The scientist comes up with a research question, generates tentative theories, deduces specific predictions to test those theories through experimentation, carries out the experiment, makes a judgement based on the result, and then repeats if necessary. This is what we might call the "traditional" view of what constitutes science practice.

However, as we've described above, both deductive and inductive thinking abilities are necessary. Also, we need to understand better what kind of thinking goes into determining research questions, creating

Figure 1.2 Schematic representation of the traditional "scientific method"

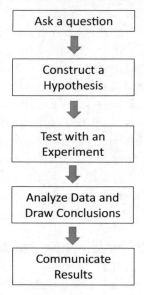

hypotheses, designing experiments, and making judgements. Some of this is embedded in the "scientific method" shown in Figure 1.2. However, a lot of really important stuff is missing. Pattern recognition. Thinking about causation. How do you determine the relevant aspects and then design a fair test? What do I use to make a judgement and can I estimate the value of the evidence, and therefore my confidence in my judgement?

Figure 1.3 shows a more representative model of the scientific method adapted from my book *Creating Scientists*. It shows a more complex view of the practice of science with a guide to how the reasoning patterns I've described above fit into the process. Specifically, the thin bordered text boxes in Figure 1.3 highlight the eight essential practices of science that all students should learn, as detailed in my book *Creating Scientists* and in the NGSS and *Framework* (National Research Council, 2012; NGSS Lead States, 2013; Moore, 2017). I have separated these practices into three dimensions:

1. investigation,
2. interpretation
3. communication

Figure 1.3 A more accurate model of how the scientist practices science

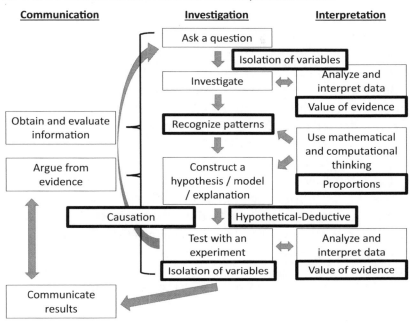

The thick bordered text boxes show the six science thinking patterns. Combined, Figure 1.3 is a basic guide to how science thinking patterns and practices fit together within the total science process.

You'll notice that, in reality, the scientific method is more complex and fluid than we've been led to believe by textbooks. Furthermore, the practices and thinking themselves don't have easily identifiable "borders." An observation leading to a recognizable pattern necessarily becomes a lesson in argument from evidence and explanation construction, which are practices we discussed in great detail in *Creating Scientists*. Working in a team to develop and use a model often requires abilities in analyzing data and using mathematics.

Also, good science thinking is necessary to successfully perform the science practices. Coming up with a hypothesis requires pattern recognition. Thinking proportionally is a necessary component of mathematical and computational thinking. When the scientist analyzes data, they must constantly evaluate the reliability and validity of the data. In reality, the practices and thinking are completely intertwined, further highlighting the necessity for three-dimensional teaching and student learning across all three dimensions at the same time.

Summary

In this chapter, I have tried to answer the question: "what is science thinking?" To this end, we have discussed how experts do science, the practices they employ, and the ways they think about science. I have briefly described the research into the ways students view science, the wide gulf between the student and the expert, and how "traditional" teaching can actually reinforce novice views of science and novice-like thinking. I have also reviewed the research literature where smart people have debated the meaning of the phrase "science thinking." Putting this all together, I have synthesized a fairly simple framework for you to use in the classroom, outlining seven science thinking patterns that you can develop in your students' minds. In the next chapter, we'll see how these thinking patterns are integrated into new standards. Throughout the rest of the book, we'll look at specific strategies for teaching and assessing thinking.

The following is a brief summary of the key points:

- ◆ Science thinking is defined as the type of thinking that scientists do.
- ◆ Students view science as a collection of facts, with the principle learning method for science being memorization.
- ◆ We can accidentally reinforce this novice view if we are not careful.
- ◆ Real science is tentative, ever expanding, and utilizes practices/methods that are cross-cutting across disciplines.
- ◆ We can introduce students to science thinking through the following seven thinking patterns:

  - ◇ Pattern recognition
  - ◇ Causation
  - ◇ Determining relevant variables and isolating them
  - ◇ Hypothetical-deductive thinking
  - ◇ Metacognition and the relative value of evidence
  - ◇ Proportional thinking.

- ◆ The practice of science and science thinking are intertwined.
- ◆ For true understanding, all three dimensions are necessary: *knowing, doing,* and *thinking*. To teach true understanding, you must teach three-dimensionally.

References

Adams, W. K., Perkins, K. K., S., P. N., Dubson, M., Finkelstein, N. D., & Wieman, C. E. (2006). New instrument for measuring student beliefs about physics and learning physics: The Colorado Learning Attitudes about Science Survey. *Physical Review Special Topics – Physics Education Research, 2*(1).

Allchin, D. (2003). Lawson's Shoehorn, or Should the Philosophy of Science Be Rated X? *Science and Education, 12,* 315–329.

Edmondson, K. M., & Novak, J. D. (1993). The interplay of scientific epistemological views, learning strategies, and attitudes of college students. *Journal of Research in Science Teaching, 30,* 547–559.

Hestenes, I., & Halloun, D. (1996). Views About Sciences Survey. *Annual Meeting of the National Association for Research in Science Teaching.* Saint Louis, MI: ERIC Document No. ED394840.

Hestenes, I., & Halloun, D. (1998). Interpreting VASS Dimensions and Profiles. *Science & Education, 7*(6), 553–577.

Holyoak, K., & Morrison, R. (2005). *Thinking and Reasoning: A Reader's Guide.* Cambridge, UK: Cambridge University Press.

Kuhn, D. (2004). What is scientific thinking and how does it develop? In U. Goswami (ed.), *Blackwell Handbook of Childhood Cognitive Development* (pp. 371–393). Malden, MA: Wiley-Blackwell.

Latour, B. (1987). *Science in Action: How to Follow Scientists and Engineers through Society.* Milton Keynes, UK: Open University Press.

Lawson, A. E. (1982). The nature of advanced reasoning and science instruction. *Journal of Research in Science Teaching, 19,* 743.

Lawson, A. E. (2005). What is the role of induction and deduction in reasoning and scientific inquiry? *Journal of Research in Science Teaching, 42,* 716–740.

Moore, C. (2017). *Creating Scientists: Teaching and Assessing Science Practice for the NGSS.* New York, NY: Routledge.

Moore, J. C. (2012). Transitional to Formal Operational: Using Authentic Research Experiences to Get Non-Science Students to Think More Like Scientists. *European Journal of Physics Education, 3*(4).

National Research Council. (2012). *A Framework for K-12 Science Education: Practices, Crosscutting Concepts, and Core Ideas.* Washington, DC: The National Academies Press.

NGSS Lead States. (2013). *Next Generation Science Standards: For States, By States.* Washington, DC: The National Academies Press.

Overton, W. F. (1990). *Reasoning, Necessity, and Logic: Developmental Perspectives.* Hillsdale, NJ: Lawrence Erlbaum Assoc.

Shan, K. J. (2013). Improving student learning and views of physics in a large enrollment introductory physics class. *Theses and Dissertations, 205.*

Tsai, C.-C. (1998). An analysis of scientific epistemological beliefs and learning orientations of Taiwanese eighth graders. *Science Education, 82*(4), 473–489.

2

How Is Science Thinking Integrated into Next Generation Standards?

"Crosscutting concepts . . . provide students with connections and intellectual tools that are related across the differing areas of disciplinary content and can enrich their application of practices and their understanding of core ideas."
—*A Framework for K–12 Education* (National Research Council, 2012)

In this chapter, we will see how knowing, doing, and thinking are incorporated into emerging science standards around the world, with a specific focus on the NGSS in the USA. Although the primary audience for this book is USA-based teachers, the three-dimensional principles discussed are universal. Science standards around the world are changing and are beginning to be aligned with the cognitive science on understanding we discussed in the last chapter. For readers in the USA, those standards are here in the form of the NGSS, and are beginning to be implemented in the various states, sometimes using different names such as Nebraska's College and Career Ready Science Standards (NCCRSS, introduced in late 2017).

I will provide a short review of what the NGSS are, their foundation, and how knowing, doing, and thinking are tightly integrated within the standards. I'll show you some examples of NGSS performance expectations and highlight how all of them take the same basic form: doing science with appropriate thinking to know content. We'll briefly review the three dimensions that make up the standards: disciplinary core ideas (DCIs), science practices, and crosscutting concepts. Although many new sets of state-specific standards differ in some ways from the NGSS, most states have or are in the process of adopting new science standards having a similar three-dimensional framework.

For the purposes of this book, I will focus on what the *Framework* and the NGSS call "crosscutting concepts." We'll see how these crosscutting concepts align with the science thinking patterns we identify from the research literature in Chapter 1. The idea behind crosscutting concepts and science thinking are actually different at their base. However, they significantly overlap, with many of the thinking patterns fitting seamlessly into the crosscutting concepts. We'll see where they overlap and where they don't and discuss the fundamental differences.

Finally, we'll talk about why there is so much overlap between the two ideas. Crosscutting concepts are a set of connections and intellectual tools that are related across science disciplines. The science thinking patterns we discussed in Chapter 1 are defined as those thinking abilities utilized by all scientists, no matter their specific discipline. They're also crosscutting. It's not terribly surprising that there would be overlap. It turns out, we can think of science thinking as a sub-component of the crosscutting concepts, with a few cross-disciplinary content-based ideas rounding out the set. With that said, other than a couple of instances, science thinking isn't *explicitly* built into the standards. In Chapter 3, we'll discuss why you will need to be explicit with respect to science thinking in your classroom, whether or not the NGSS is.

What Are the Next Generation Science Standards?

The NGSS was the result of a collaboration between 26 states, the National Science Teachers Association, the American Association for the Advancement of Science, the National Research Council, and the non-profit Achieve, Incorporated. The standards are based on the National Research Council's *Framework*, as described in the introduction. According to the resulting documents, the goal of the NGSS writing team was to create new science standards that were "rich in content and practice, arranged in a coherent manner across disciplines and grades to provide all students an internationally benchmarked science education" (NGSS Lead States, 2013). The standards were released in April 2013.

The NGSS center around three dimensions of teaching and learning: the DCIs, science practices, and crosscutting concepts. DCIs are the basic content the writing team expects an educated citizenry to understand across the physical, chemical, and natural sciences. Identified within the NGSS are eight science practices that cross disciplines and grade-levels. Table 2.1 shows these practices, which I have separated into three categories: 1. investigation, 2. interpretation, and 3. communication, discussed in greater detail in *Creating Scientists* (Moore, 2017; NGSS Lead States, 2013). Finally, the crosscutting concepts are a set of connections and intellectual tools that are related across science disciplines (NGSS Lead States, 2013). Within the NGSS, all of the components of the three dimensions are consistent across the grade levels, where students are expected to build on and revise knowledge as they progress through the grade levels and acquire greater sophistication in content, science practice, and cognitive ability.

Figure 2.1 shows how the three NGSS dimensions align with the three dimensions of understanding that we discussed in Chapter 1. The DCIs

TABLE 2.1 SCIENCE PRACTICES IDENTIFIED IN THE *FRAMEWORK* (NATIONAL RESEARCH COUNCIL, 2012). THESE PRACTICES HAVE BEEN SEPARATED INTO THREE CATEGORIES: INVESTIGATION, INTERPRETATION, AND COMMUNICATION (MOORE, 2017)

Category	Science practice
Investigation	Ask questions and define problems Develop and use models Plan and carry out investigations
Interpretation	Analyze and interpret data Use mathematics and computational thinking Construct explanations and design solutions
Communication	Engage in argument from evidence Obtain, evaluate, and communicate information

Figure 2.1 How the NGSS dimensions roughly align with our knowing-doing-thinking model for understanding

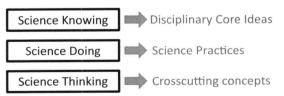

outline the science content we want students to know. The set of eight science practices shown in Table 2.1 outline what it is we want our students to be able to do. The seven crosscutting concepts roughly outline how we want our students to think across the various disciplines. As we'll see later in the chapter, the science thinking patterns listed in the previous chapter don't directly align with crosscutting concepts, but the alignment is close enough for our immediate discussion.

Before the NGSS, most science standards at the individual state and district levels, along with standard science education practices, separated the three dimensions, if they were taught at all. Specifically, science practice performance expectations (sometimes called student learning outcomes) would be separate from content expectations, with specific science thinking patterns typically left implied instead of being outlined explicitly. Although not necessarily the intention, this separation had the practical effect of each dimension being taught and assessed individually.

Let us look at the following two generalized performance expectations:

The student will be able to:

1. Demonstrate an understanding of [content].
2. Graph the relationship between an independent and dependent variable.

The first expectation is easily "assessed" using the ages-old standardized multiple-choice test, in many cases requiring little more than rote memorization to master. Whether actual understanding is achieved and whether the assessment is accurately measuring understanding is debatable. (Within our *knowing-doing-thinking* framework, it doesn't.) The second expectation can be assessed by examination of a student's work completing the task. The context of the task is irrelevant to the expectation. To the teacher, these two performance expectations signify two separate lessons. One on content, the next on graphs. Maybe the graphs lesson happens sometime later in the academic year, so long as it eventually happens. Notice there is no explicit focus on thinking such as pattern recognition or scales/proportions, both of which would be necessary to authentically construct a graphical representation from data.

We know from Chapter 1 that within the actual performance of science these dimensions are intimately linked, as opposed to separate chunks of stuff done out of context. Studies of expert/novice practice demonstrate that cognitive abilities are not independent of content, experience, or environment

(Kuhn, 2004). A learner best deploys practices and demonstrates thinking within context, where content learning, practice, and thinking are interrelated. Basically, if we want to immerse our students in authentic science, then we must not separate the knowing from the doing and thinking.

The NGSS Are Three-Dimensional

In contrast to past standards, the NGSS tightly integrates the three dimensions. The NGSS were designed based off of the *Framework*, which itself was based on the research done in situated cognition theory and application (National Research Council, 2012). This becomes obvious when we look at how the NGSS performance expectations are written. The following is a basic model for how each of the performance expectations are written in the NGSS:

Students who demonstrate understanding can:

1. construct an argument supported by empirical evidence to support . . . [content]
2. develop a model based on evidence to illustrate . . . [content]
3. analyze and interpret data on the . . . [content]
4. construct, use, and present arguments to support the claim that . . . [content]
5. conduct an investigation to provide evidence that . . . [content]

Each of these shorter segments is followed by some specific content, but the beginning is similar across *all* content for each grade level. From this we can really start to see the tight integration of knowing, doing, and thinking within the NGSS.

Here's the general formula:

Students who demonstrate understanding . . .
    can perform science practice . . .
    using appropriate science thinking . . .
    in pursuit of content.

One of the eight science practices shown in Table 2.1 and one of the six thinking patterns shown in Table 1.2 are used by the student in their discovery of whatever content we are interested in teaching that day. You can't make a peanut butter and jelly sandwich without peanut butter, jelly, *and* bread. You can't teach science understanding without content, practice, *and* thinking. Chapter 1 taught us that students *can only understand* science ideas if they understand how to practice science in context. Merely "knowing" some science fact does not in itself signify understanding, no more than being able to repeat that the stove is hot signifies understanding of hotness in the mind of the child. The NGSS recognizes this interrelationship.

Now, let's look at some examples of full performance expectations from the NGSS. Table 2.2 shows examples of performance expectations for each of the eight science practices detailed in Table 2.1 (NGSS Lead States, 2013). Furthermore, I highlight some of the thinking patterns we discussed in the previous chapter by underlining them as they appear in the performance expectations.

TABLE 2.2 EXAMPLES OF NGSS PERFORMANCE EXPECTATIONS FOR EACH SCIENCE PRACTICE (NGSS LEAD STATES, 2013). SCIENCE THINKING WITHIN THE PERFORMANCE EXPECTATIONS ARE UNDERLINED

Science practice	Example NGSS performance expectation
Ask questions and define problems	3-PS2–3. Ask questions to determine cause and effect relationships of electric or magnetic interactions between two objects not in contact with each other. MS-PS2–3. Ask questions about data to determine the factors that affect the strength of electric and magnetic forces.
Develop and use models	5-PS1–1. Develop a model to describe that matter is made of particles too small to be seen. MS-PS1–1. Develop models to describe the atomic composition of simple molecules and extended structures. HS-PS1–1. Use the periodic table as a model to predict the relative properties of elements based on the patterns of electrons in the outermost energy level of atoms.
Plan and carry out investigations	1-PS4–1. Plan and conduct investigations to provide evidence that vibrating materials can make sound and that sound can make materials vibrate. MS-LS1–1. Conduct an investigation to provide evidence that living things are made of cells; either one cell or many different numbers and types of cells. HS-PS2–5. Plan and conduct an investigation to provide evidence that an electric current can produce a magnetic field and that a changing magnetic field can produce an electric current.
Analyze and interpret data	K-ESS2–1. Use and share observations of local weather conditions to describe patterns over time. 3-ESS2–1. Represent data in tables and graphical displays to describe typical weather conditions expected during a particular season. HS-ESS2–2. Analyze geoscience data to make the claim that one change to Earth's surface can create feedbacks that cause changes to other Earth systems.

(Continued)

TABLE 2.2 (CONTINUED)

Science practice	Example NGSS performance expectation
Use mathematics and computational thinking	5-PS1–2. Measure and graph quantities <u>to provide evidence</u> that regardless of the type of change that occurs when heating, cooling, or mixing substances, the total weight of matter is conserved. HS-PS1–7. Use mathematical representations <u>to support the claim</u> that atoms, and therefore mass, are conserved during a chemical reaction. HS-ESS1–4. Use mathematical or computational representations <u>to predict</u> the motion of orbiting objects in the solar system.
Construct explanations and design solutions	1-PS4–2. Make observations <u>to construct an evidence-based account</u> that objects in darkness can be seen only when illuminated. MS-PS3–3. Apply scientific principles to design, construct, and test a device that either minimizes or maximizes thermal energy transfer. HS-PS1–5. Apply scientific principles and evidence <u>to provide an explanation</u> about the effects of changing the temperature or concentration of the reacting particles on the rate at which a reaction occurs.
Engage in argument from evidence	2-PS1–4. Construct an argument with <u>evidence that some changes</u> caused by heating or cooling can be reversed and some cannot. MS-PS2–4. Construct and present arguments using evidence <u>to support the claim</u> that gravitational interactions are attractive and depend on the masses of interacting objects. HS-PS4–3. <u>Evaluate</u> the claims, evidence, and reasoning behind the idea that electromagnetic radiation can be described either by a wave model or a particle model, and that for some situations one model is more useful than the other.
Obtain, evaluate, and communicate information	2-ESS2–3. Obtain information <u>to identify</u> where water is found on Earth and that it can be solid or liquid. MS-PS1–3. Gather and <u>make sense</u> of information <u>to describe</u> that synthetic materials come from natural resources and impact society. HS-PS4–4. <u>Evaluate the validity and reliability of claims</u> in published materials of the effects that different frequencies of electromagnetic radiation have when absorbed by matter.

The performance expectation in the NGSS are labeled as follows:

GRADE LEVEL – DISCIPLINARY CORE IDEA – PERFORMANCE EXPECTATION

As an example, the first performance expectation listed in Table 2.2 is the following:

3-PS2–3.   Ask questions to determine cause and effect relationships of electric or magnetic interactions between two objects not in contact with each other.

From the code that precedes each performance expectation, you can tell that this one is for the 3rd grade, is within the domain of physical science

TABLE 2.3 DISSECTING A NGSS PERFORMANCE EXPECTATIONS INTO THE DIMENSIONS OF DOING, THINKING, AND KNOWING

	Specific dimension	Performance expectation
Doing	Ask questions and define problems	Ask questions . . .
Thinking	Causative thinking	to determine cause and effect relationships . . .
Knowing	Forces and interactions	of electric or magnetic interactions between two objects not in contact with each other.

(PS), and focuses on DCI PS2 (forces, motion, and types of interactions). It is the third performance expectation within this group. Similarly, a code of MS-PS3–3 would correspond to the middle school age group, physical science, and DCI PS3 (Energy). You can find a listing of all of the DCIs and how they progress across age groups in *APPENDIX E – Progressions Within the Next Generation Science Standards* listed in the references section of this chapter (NGSS Lead States, 2013).

Table 2.3 shows performance expectation 3-PS2–3 broken down into its three dimensions. The science practice of asking questions and defining problems is the means students will use to achieve understanding of magnetic and electric interactions. Specifically, the student will need to use causative thinking to determine a cause/effect relationship for magnetic and electric interactions. The fundamental content knowledge being learned with all of this doing and thinking is the concept of force and how objects can interact without touching.

Science Thinking In the NGSS

We spent all of Chapter 1 coming up with a pretty good definition of science thinking by scouring the research literature, culminating in the six science thinking patterns detailed in Table 1.2. However, the NGSS doesn't explicitly outline these specific thinking patterns. Instead, the third dimension of teaching and learning within the NGSS is what are called "crosscutting concepts." The idea behind crosscutting concepts and science thinking are actually somewhat different. However, they do significantly overlap, with many of the thinking patterns fitting seamlessly into the crosscutting concepts.

Table 2.4 details all seven of the crosscutting concepts identified in the NGSS. They are as follows with descriptions quoted from the *Framework* (NGSS Lead States, 2013b; National Research Council, 2012):

1. Patterns
2. Cause and effect
3. Scale, proportion, and quantity
4. Systems and system models
5. Energy and matter
6. Structure and function
7. Stability and change.

Patterns are the foundation of science. Ultimately, science only works because nature keeps repeating itself across all domains. These patterns and individual events have causes, with a major activity of science being the investigation and explanation of these causal relationships. The patterns and relationships we observe can be critically related to different

TABLE 2.4 NGSS CROSSCUTTING CONCEPTS (NGSS LEAD STATES, 2013B)

Crosscutting concept	Description
Patterns	"Observed patterns of forms and events guide organization and classification, and they prompt questions about relationships and the factors that influence them."
Cause and Effect	"Events have causes, sometimes simple, sometimes multifaceted. A major activity of science is investigating and explaining causal relationships and the mechanisms by which they are mediated. Such mechanisms can then be tested across given contexts and used to predict and explain events in new contexts."
Scale, Proportion, and Quantity	"In considering phenomena, it is critical to recognize what is relevant at different measures of size, time, and energy and to recognize how changes in scale, proportion, or quantity affect a system's structure or performance."
Systems and System Models	"Defining the system under study – specifying its boundaries and making explicit a model of that system – provides tools for understanding and testing ideas that are applicable throughout science and engineering."
Energy and Matter	"Tracking fluxes of energy and matter into, out of, and within systems helps one understand the systems' possibilities and limitations."
Structure and Function	"The way in which an object or living thing is shaped and its substructure determine many of its properties and functions."
Stability and Change	"For natural and built systems alike, conditions of stability and determinants of rates of change or evolution of a system are critical elements of study."

Source: Descriptions are quoted from Chapter 4 of the *Framework* (National Research Council, 2012)

measures of size, time, and energy, where changes in scale, proportion, or quantity can significantly affect what we observe. These first three cross-cutting concepts have some fairly obvious overlap with several of the science thinking patterns we discussed in the previous chapter.

There are other intellectual tools used by all scientists included in the crosscutting concepts, such as the definition of systems and explicit modeling of behavior. Specifically, natural systems across all scientific domains require the tracking of changes in energy and matter. Furthermore, shapes and substructures of materials or living things can determine many of the properties and functions, as well as how energy/matter flow. Finally, how systems change over time and what causes those changes (or doesn't) is a connecting concept that bridges disciplines.

You'll note that the first three crosscutting concepts are directly related to the scientific thinking patterns of pattern recognition, causative thinking, and proportional thinking. But what about the other crosscutting concepts?

First, the idea of crosscutting concepts is fundamentally different from the idea of science thinking patterns. For the latter, we're interested in knowing what goes on inside of the scientist's head as they do science. For the former, we're describing the concepts that bridge disciplinary boundaries, with a goal of helping students deepen their understanding of science as something bigger than just physics or biology.

Let's look at an example to better understand the distinction between thinking and crosscutting concepts, and how crosscutting concepts are distinct from science practices. Imagine a biology class and a physical science class. In the biology class, students are creating a taxonomy of fish based on certain identifiable and repeatable features. In the physical science class, students are creating a taxonomy of materials based on how they magnetically interact with each other.

Looking at a collection of fish pictures and/or descriptions, the biology students might ultimately classify the fish into two categories based on whether or not the fish have bones. The physics students might divide a set of materials given to them into three group: 1. those that attract and repel each other, 2. those that are attracted to the first group but not each other, and 3. those that don't interact at all. The biology class has learned about Chondrichthyes and Osteichthyes, whereas the physical science class has defined magnets, ferromagnets, and non-magnetic materials.

Both classes are fundamentally doing the same thing: they're creating a taxonomy. This type of scientific activity is ultimately centered on the concept of patterns, and when looked at from above the content level, they both center on exactly the same concept. The concept is crosscutting.

During the activity, students will have to *do* several things, such as plan an investigation (an observation experiment), analyze the data, and finally develop a model (the taxonomy). These are the science practices that the student will *do*. The *concept* on which the activity is based is patterns in nature. The distinction between practices and crosscutting concepts is that scientists *do* practices, and crosscutting concepts are *ideas* that span disciplines.

How do crosscutting concepts differ from science thinking patterns? As our hypothetical biology and physics classes develop greater sophistication, they'll start to learn the *cause* of these distinct classifications. For example, the physical science students will eventually learn in future physics classes that the atomic and molecular structures of the materials determine whether or not a material is magnetic, ferromagnetic, or nonmagnetic. The structure determines the properties. Similarly, having muscle attached directly to an armor-like skin, like Chondrichthyes (sharks!), as opposed to internal bone has a significant mechanical advantage, resulting in less energy loss while swimming through the water. Once again, structure is seen to directly influence properties.

The *concept* that structure dictates properties is not a *thinking pattern*. It's an idea that scientists have observed over and over across all the different scientific disciplines. Highlighting this crosscutting concept in class, however, does provide a tool for the student to use as they move through the sciences. They know to be on the lookout for patterns and structure. Notice, though, that it takes the thinking pattern of *pattern recognition* to realize that there is a connection between structure and properties, and that this connection is seen over and over. Therefore, the thinking patterns are embedded in the crosscutting concepts, whether they are explicit or not.

We noticed right away that several of the crosscutting concepts are directly linked with science thinking patterns, and that the link is more subtle with others. It goes deeper, though, as science thinking patterns are also tied up with the science practices. We saw an example of this in the previous chapter, as detailed in Figure 1.3.

Let's go ahead and answer the question: how are the science thinking patterns integrated into the NGSS? Figure 2.2 is a schematic sketch of how science thinking is deeply woven into the NGSS. On the left side I have

Figure 2.2 Sketch showing how science thinking patterns are woven into the NGSS dimensions of science practices and crosscutting concepts

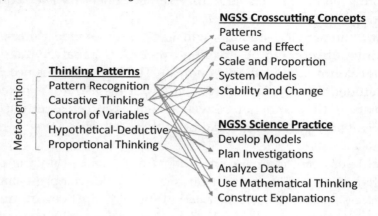

listed all of the science thinking patterns. On the right side are selected components of the science practices and crosscutting concepts in the NGSS. In between is a tangled mess of connections between the thinking patterns, practices, and crosscutting concepts.

In some cases, thinking patterns are explicit within the NGSS. For example, pattern recognition, causative thinking, and proportional thinking are built right into the crosscutting concepts. They directly represent the thinking behind patterns, cause/effect, and scale. Furthermore, these same thinking patterns are also a necessary component of successful practice. For example, pattern recognition is essential in the practice of developing models. Proportional thinking is required to successfully practice analyzing data.

Going Beyond the NGSS

Most of the six thinking patterns we identified in the previous chapter don't explicitly appear in the NGSS. That certainly doesn't mean that they aren't important. In fact, I would argue that this lack of explicit delineation of thinking patterns is a weakness of the NGSS. You'll see in the next chapter that you will have to be explicit about reasoning in your classroom if you want to successfully develop the reasoning abilities of your students.

Let's look at control of variables, as an example. Within the top-level framework of the NGSS, this specific thinking pattern isn't explicitly identified. However, it is impossible for the student to plan an investigation without explicitly thinking about relevant variables and how to isolate them during performance of the investigation. This thinking pattern is a necessary component of the practice. Similarly, the concept of cause/effect *requires* thinking about the variable that does the causing and the variable that is being affected. Without this mental recognition of variables and their relationship, there would be no meaningful concept of patterns.

It really shouldn't be surprising that thinking is so tied up with practice and knowledge. That was the entire point of Chapter 1. What I want you to recognize is that science thinking *is* an essential component of the NGSS and science learning in general. It's just not explicit, other than a few cases. With this book, I'm trying to make science thinking explicit, and to get you to be explicit about thinking in your teaching. I'm asking you to go beyond the strict written word of the standards, because you ultimately have to if you want your students to understand science.

Instead of focusing on a student's skill at using a particular instrument for the chemistry class, you will be more interested in that student's ability to evaluate and minimize the uncertainty in the temperature measurement. You will want your students to develop the ability to create a mathematical model for a given electrical circuit, and then make a prediction based on that model. Because the NGSS demands it, you will want to assess whether your students can determine what variables are important to measure.

My own research and that of cognitive scientists has shown that science thinking abilities are often required for effective decision making and problem solving far outside the typical scientific context (Reif & Larkin, 1991; Moore & Slisko, 2017). This is why I think these types of abilities are *far* more important for an educated population than their ability to recall an equation, an element on the periodic table, or the names of structures found on diagrams of the cell. The writers of the NGSS agree, which is demonstrated by the significant focus on practices. However, the thinking is critical for successful deployment of practices.

When you first start to reform your teaching by incorporating three-dimensional activities, it's probably wise to begin by specifically developing and implementing classroom activities that directly address NGSS performance expectations. However, as you grow more comfortable teaching through knowing, doing, and thinking, you'll begin to realize that the three dimensions themselves don't have easily identifiable "borders." An observation experiment leading to a recognizable pattern necessarily becomes a lesson in argument from evidence and explanation construction, all of which will take pretty much all of the thinking patterns (and maybe more). Working in a team to develop and use a model often requires abilities at analyzing data and using mathematics, which means proportional thinking at a minimum. In reality, the practices and thinking are intertwined, whether the NGSS explicitly "asks" you to intertwine them or not.

Summary

In this chapter, we discussed how knowing, doing, and thinking are incorporated into emerging science standards around the world, with a specific focus on the NGSS in the USA. Specifically, I provided a short review of what the NGSS are, their foundation, and how knowing, doing, and thinking are tightly integrated within the standards. We outlined the three dimensions that make up the standards: DCIs, science practices, and crosscutting concepts.

We saw that NGSS crosscutting concepts align with the science thinking patterns we identified from the research literature in Chapter 1. Crosscutting concepts and science thinking are actually fundamentally different. However, they significantly overlap, with many of the thinking patterns fitting seamlessly into the crosscutting concepts. We learned that crosscutting concepts are a set of *ideas* that are related across science disciplines. Science thinking patterns describe what goes on in the scientist mind in the moment.

The main take-away from this chapter is that the NGSS doesn't explicitly outline science thinking. It is incorporated throughout the science practices and crosscutting concepts. However, thinking patterns are essential for performing the practices successfully, and ultimately for understanding science.

The following is a brief summary of the main points:

- ◆ The NGSS consist of the following three dimensions:
  - ◇ Disciplinary core ideas,
  - ◇ Science practices, and
  - ◇ Crosscutting concepts.
- ◆ These three dimensions roughly align with our three-dimensional model for understanding:
  - ◇ Knowing,
  - ◇ Thinking, and
  - ◇ Doing.

- ◆ Disciplinary core ideas are the content learned through activity.
- ◆ Science practices are actions that students do in the process of learning.
- ◆ Crosscutting concepts are common ideas that are found across all science disciplines.
- ◆ Science thinking is woven throughout both the science practices and the crosscutting concepts.
- ◆ The NGSS aren't explicit about science thinking, but science thinking is critical to working with the NGSS.

References

Kuhn, D. (2004). What is scientific thinking and how does it develop? In U. Goswami (ed.), *Blackwell Handbook of Childhood Cognitive Development*. Malden, MA: Wiley-Blackwell.

Moore, C. (2017). *Creating Scientists: Teaching and Assessing Science Practice for the NGSS*. New York, NY: Routledge.

Moore, J. C., & Slisko, J. (2017). Dynamic Visualizations of Multi-body Physics Problems and Scienrtic Reasoning: A Threshold to Understanding. In T. Greczylo, & E. Debowska (eds), *Key Competences in Physics Teaching and Learning*. New York, NY: Springer.

National Research Council. (2012). *A Framework for K-12 Science Education: Practices, Crosscutting Concepts, and Core Ideas*. Washington, DC: The National Academies Press.

NGSS Lead States. (2013). *Next Generation Science Standards: For States, By States*. Washington, DC: The National Academies Press.

Reif, F., & Larkin, J. H. (1991). Cognition in scientific and everyday domains: Comparisons and learning implications. *Research in Science Teaching, 28*, 733.

3

How Do You Teach and Assess Science Thinking?

"Telling children how scientists do science does not necessarily lead to far-reaching changes in how children do science."

—Seymour Papert (Papert, 1991)

In Chapter 1, we learned that students can only understand science by knowing, doing, and thinking in the science classroom. In Chapter 2, we saw how national standards in the USA have been changing to incorporate this fuller definition of understanding, with special emphasis on developing abilities in deep scientific thinking. In this chapter, we'll focus on what you, the teacher, can do in your classroom to facilitate this knowing, doing, and thinking. In particular, we'll discuss the absolute necessity of being explicit with respect to reasoning.

A shift in focus from traditional descriptive content knowledge towards an integration of knowledge, practice, and reasoning requires a similar shift in pedagogy. What pedagogies lead to demonstrated improvements in science thinking abilities? The NGSS is purposefully agnostic on pedagogy, so we'll have to look to the research literature to see what has worked, and maybe more importantly, what has not worked. Then, we'll have to synthesize the literature into a workable framework for creating new lessons that meet the needs of your classroom. Specifically, we'll discuss *apprenticeship* as a model for teaching science thinking, and see how apprenticeship is both similar and different from what you might know as inquiry-based teaching. I'll try my best to reduce the thousands of pages of writing on apprenticeship in the science classroom to an easily remembered and applicable mantra you can use to focus teaching in your classroom.

Probably the biggest takeaway from this chapter will be that you absolutely must make science thinking count in your classroom if you want your students to take science thinking seriously. I'll discuss research-verified methods for doing that, with focus on monitoring and assessing the student in their deployment of science thinking patterns. To prepare you for the classroom-tested lessons in the next section of this book, I'll show you the process we use to build an entire assessable curriculum based on standards. What are our learning goals with respect to science thinking? What will we do in the classroom to achieve those goals? How will we know whether or not we were successful?

Part II of this book contains chapters that focus on teaching and assessing individual scientific reasoning patterns, going into greater depth on what those patterns are and what activities that develop them look like. We'll continually refer back to this chapter and the lessons it teaches. Part III of this book will go through a simple example of building an assessable, standards-based learning progression on a topic in physical science, where all of the thinking patterns make an appearance. Therefore, the chapter you're reading right now will set the teaching framework on which we will build the rest of the book.

Apprenticeships in Science

Physics education specialist Frederik Reif and cognitive scientist Jill Larkin highlight in their work that formal schooling in science typically does not resemble the actual practice of science by scientists (Reif & Larkin, 1991). Furthermore, the types of student thinking necessary to be successful in the science class aren't the same as the thinking necessary to be successful in the science laboratory. We need to change that by making our classroom activities more closely mirror authentic science, and assessing our students based on authentic science thinking.

In Chapter 1 we learned about *situated cognition*, which is the theory of learning where understanding requires the three dimensions of knowing, doing, and thinking. *Cognitive apprenticeship* is a theory of teaching that builds on situated cognition to produce a strong framework for the teaching and learning of science, where students learn by doing "at the elbows of experts" (Barab & Hay, 2001).

Most of you reading this book have some experience and/or knowledge about the basic concept of apprenticeship. After all, student teaching is a type of workplace apprenticeship where the apprentice learns processes through physical integration into the practices associated with the content area (Pratt, 1998). As an example, the teaching "apprentice" works side-by-side with a master teacher who shows them the realities of the profession. The student teacher learns by watching an expert, then by designing and leading lessons under the supervision of the expert. As the student teacher gains more and more abilities, the master teacher allows more and more freedom to work until they are eventually practicing on their own.

Cognitive apprenticeship borrows from traditional apprenticeship as an applied teaching technique for students constrained to the classroom. In this framework for teaching, we are really doing a *simulated* apprenticeship (Barab & Hay, 2001). Research across many different disciplines has shown that simulating expert-like practice in context and in an aided environment can increase student abilities in an unaided setting (Ghefaili, 2003).

The principal teaching methods of cognitive apprenticeship are summarized in Table 3.1 (Brown, Collins, & Duguid, 1989; Moore, 2017). *Modeling*, *coaching*, and *scaffolding* are the principal teaching methods directly facilitated by the instructor. They are designed to help students construct a conceptual model for science content and develop a set of cognitive abilities through the practice of science. *Reflection* and *articulation* serve to internalize the student's observations and experience, as well as aid in integrating new knowledge, problem-solving skills, and thinking abilities. Finally, *exploration* fosters independence and encourages autonomous problem formulations and solutions.

Inquiry-based learning is a pedagogical technique compatible with cognitive apprenticeship where lessons are framed as a question, a problem, or some sort of investigation, as opposed to the teaching-by-telling process of descriptions and/or explanations of "facts." Fundamentally, inquiry is a "constructivist" pedagogy, where students construct their own knowledge and make meaning of it based on personal experiences (Bachtold, 2013). Students actively participate in the development of the new knowledge by participating in authentic activities (Roth & Jornet, 2013).

TABLE 3.1 THE PRINCIPLE METHODS OF COGNITIVE APPRENTICESHIP

Method	Description
Modeling	A subject expert explicitly demonstrates a task to the student. The student is able to build a conceptual model for the task. Implicit processes are exposed so that the student can observe and understand the rationale for the process.
Coaching	The expert observes the student attempting a task and gives them feedback and assistance at critical moments. Students are actively involved in the process and are required to integrate sub-abilities and conceptual knowledge.
Scaffolding	The expert assists the student in performing a task, specifically in areas where the student's abilities are still novice-like. Assistance is slowly withdrawn as the student gains new abilities and can manage more of the task on their own.
Reflection	The student reflects on their own performance in solving a problem through analysis and deconstruction. The student can increase their self-awareness of knowledge and compare their own understanding and performance with that of their peers and the expert.
Articulation	The student thinks about their own actions and explains them to others, making their knowledge explicit. This allows the student to reorganize their knowledge and generalize its application to related problems.
Exploration	In exploration, students investigate new methods, strategies, and test new hypotheses by exploring the problem. Students can set their own goals and develop their own testing strategies, all of which fosters independent learning.

Source: Brown, et al., 1989

Heather Banchi and Randy Bell outline the four levels of inquiry, which I have provided for you in Table 3.2 (Banchi & Bell, 2008; Moore, 2017). In the same table, I also show how these ideas of inquiry seamlessly integrate with the principle teaching techniques in cognitive apprenticeship of modeling, coaching, scaffolding, and exploration. The levels of inquiry progress from completely teacher-supplied exploration, where the research question, science practices, procedure, and result are all given, to complete open exploration, where the student supplies all of these things.

From Table 3.2, we see that inquiry-based learning is a method in science teaching that fits nicely within cognitive apprenticeship. However, notice that reflection and articulation are not explicitly built into the inquiry framework. In the typical inquiry-based science lesson, the first three methods of cognitive apprenticeship are often present, with poor implementations forgetting to incorporate the others. You can probably guess from their descriptions that the final three are absolutely *critical* for developing scientific thinking! Reflection, articulation, and exploration don't happen on their own in the science classroom. They must be explicitly incorporated into your instruction.

TABLE 3.2 HOW THE LEVELS OF INQUIRY WITHIN INQUIRY-BASED LEARNING FIT WITHIN THE FRAMEWORK OF COGNITIVE APPRENTICESHIP

Methods in cognitive apprenticeship	Levels of inquiry
Modeling	*Confirmation inquiry*: the teacher develops an activity that uses science practice to guide the student to the discovery of already known content.
Coaching	*Structured inquiry*: The teacher provides a question, the science practice to be used, and possibly the procedure that guide the student to discover new content.
Scaffolding	*Guided inquiry*: The teacher provides only the question, expecting the student to decide on the proper practices and specific procedures. Assistance is provided and slowly removed.
Exploration	*Open exploration*: The student provides the research question, the science practices to be used, the procedure and the procedure.

Source: Levels of inquiry are taken from Banchi & Bell, 2008

We'll see that these components are absolutely critical in the development of practice and thinking abilities. I want to be very clear: doing hands-on science in the classroom is not all it takes for students to be doing inquiry-based learning within the framework of cognitive apprenticeship. Not all inquiry-based lessons are good cognitive apprenticeship. For example, if you approach inquiry as merely a process to teach and reinforce content, which is possible, then even though your activities might be considered inquiry, you are not doing cognitive apprenticeship and you will not achieve gains in practice and thinking abilities.

For some evidence of this, I want to point you to some of the research. Barbara White and John Frederiksen found that middle school students studying physical science through an inquiry-based approach did measurably improve on content-based knowledge assessments. However, when students were assessed on their understanding of the inquiry process, these students demonstrated little improvement (White & Frederiksen, 1998). Lisa Blank found that seventh-grade students studying ecology through a research-based pedagogy did gain an above-average knowledge of content, albeit with little to no corresponding "restructuring of their ecology understandings" (Blank, 2000). My own research has shown that inquiry-based best-practices with respect to learning gains in content knowledge can fail to result in measurable gains in scientific thinking (Moore & Rubbo, 2012; Moore, 2012).

What is it that we are missing, then, if so-called "doing science" doesn't necessarily improve a student's ability to do science and think like a scientist? As we learned in Chapter 1, one of the defining differences between the science expert and novice is what Deanna Kuhn calls an "epistemological appreciation" of how new knowledge is formed (Kuhn, 2004). The major distinction between the novice and the expert is in the way they think about and view science and its practice. The expert consistently evaluates their own thinking and utilizes multiple resources towards solving a problem, making an observation, coming up with a hypothesis, and conducting experiments. The novice is typically "stuck" in one type of framing and rarely evaluates their own reasoning (Edmondson & Novak, 1993). Therefore, we find that metacognition, the simple act of thinking about thinking, is a defining thinking pattern of the expert scientist. Look back at Figure 2.2 to see how we schematically represented metacognition within the hierarchy of science thinking. Good science thinking *requires* metacognition at all stages.

In fact, physical science education experts Eugenia Etkina and Jose Mestre identify the importance of metacognition as one of the key, defining insights about the student that we can get from science education research (Etkina & Mestre, 2004). Specifically, when the science instruction the student is receiving doesn't fit the student's mental model for what science is, then it becomes easy for them to disengage from the course, believing that what they are doing is not important to learning. If the student expects to passively receive facts, as we've seen they do, then the guided-inquiry activity can seem to them like play-time that doesn't really hurt, but doesn't necessarily lead to any real learning about science.

Somehow, we need to get the student "in the game." It's not enough for the student to physically participate in the act of doing science. They have to mentally reflect on what it is they are doing in order to see how the practice and thinking is the means by which we know this stuff to be true.

Be Explicit. Be Reflective. Make It Count.

As discussed earlier, White and Frederiksen found little improvement in the science practice abilites of their middle-school physical science students using an inquiry-based approach. However, when they added a significant metacognitive component to instruction that they call "Reflective Assessment," students perfromed significantly better on practice and reasoning (White & Frederiksen, 1998). Similarly, Blank showed that incorporating discussions on the metacognitive aspects of the lesson improved three-dimensional understanding of ecology among middle-school biology students (Blank, 2000). My own research group found that making science thinking patterns explicit during instruction and including significant formal opportunities for students to reflect on their thinking both during and after activities has resulted in significant improvement in science thinking (Moore, 2012).

It appears that explicit instruction in thinking is really necessary for teaching thinking effectively. Biologist Anton Lawson makes clear the necessity to be explicit in instruction of scientific reasoning, specifically when having students design experiments to test hypotheses (Lawson, 2000). Etkina's and Mestre's excellent review of the research identified several instructional principles for effective three-dimensional teaching, one of which was the explicit teaching of metacognitive strategies so that students learn how to learn and how to think (Etkina & Mestre, 2004).

Etkina and Mestre go into great detail, outlining nine instructional principles synthesized from the available research in science teaching and learning. The nine principles are shown in Table 3.3. You should definitely read their work by finding the reference at the end of this chapter. I have broken these principles down into three easy to remember basic principles for reforming your teaching towards the development of science thinking abilities:

1. be explicit,
2. be reflective, and
3. make it count.

TABLE 3.3 THE NINE INSTRUCTIONAL PRINCIPLES ETKINA AND MESTRE IDENTIFY FROM A REVIEW OF RESEARCH IN SCIENCE TEACHING AND LEARNING (ETKINA & MESTRE, 2004). I HAVE BROKEN THESE PRINCIPLES DOWN INTO THREE, EASY TO REMEMBER, CATEGORIES

Be explicit	"Metacognitive strategies should be taught so that students learn how to learn." "Helping students organize content knowledge according to some hierarchy should be a priority."
Be reflective	"Construction and sense-making of science knowledge should be encouraged." "Qualitative reasoning based on concepts should be encouraged." "Hypothetico-deductive reasoning should be encouraged." "Ample opportunities should be available for learning 'the processes of doing science'"
Make it count	"Formative assessment should be used frequently to monitor students' understanding and to help tailor instruction to meet students' needs." "Ample opportunities should be provided for students to apply their knowledge flexibly across multiple contexts." "Motivation is an important factor."

The research is fairly clear on this: in order for students to pick up on the thinking patterns you have them doing in your activities, you must be explicit about what it is that they are doing. Tell them what thinking patterns they are going to use, show them how to use that thinking pattern, and guide them in their execution. Both during and after the activity, students need to reflect on what it is they are doing and what they are thinking. It is your job to ensure this is happening. And finally, students need to believe that what they are doing matters. Therefore, you must make it very clear to students that you find science thinking to be important. You can tell them this, but the best way is to show them by making science thinking count. That is to say, make science thinking at least as important to their grade as content knowledge.

Curriculum and Assessment: A Framework for Making It Count

Now, let's talk about incorporating these three ideas into your curriculum design. What specifically do you do when developing your curriculum to make it explicit, reflective, and make thinking count? When done correctly, the development of assessment and curriculum go hand-in-hand. In order to assess science thinking, you must first know how to build a curriculum that incorporates science thinking. To that end, I'll briefly describe an approach I detail in my book *Creating Scientists* that I call a hybrid product/process approach to curriculum (Smith, 2000; Moore, 2017).

The traditional product-based curriculum development theorist Ralph Tyler describes a systematic framework for developing learning, where learning objectives are set, a plan of action is determined and put into place, and the "products" are measured (Tyler, 1949). Curriculum theorist Hilda Taba even synthesized a checklist-like procedure for product-based curriculum development (Taba, 1962).

Like the limited deductive-based scientific method we discussed in Chapter 1, we must also be careful with taking strict procedural approaches to the practice of teaching. In particular, when we set the entire curriculum including assessments before day one of instruction, then we leave the learner out of the process all together. They participate in activities we design, but they have little say in the actual learning process. Furthermore, feedback they provide via assessments play no role in future instruction. This approach also has the effect of forcing a focus on the individual "products" themselves, instead of a consistent learning experience, which can minimize learning that happens outside of pre-defined products.

The practical effect of curriculum as products is the breaking down of learning into smaller and smaller units, where the teacher is faced with an avalanche of stuff to teach and assess and little to no flexibility. More recent research shows that curriculums based on products, or strict "learning objectives," are rarely actually implemented in this way, anyway (Cornbleth, 1990). This isn't necessarily a failure of the teacher, but possibly a failure of the framework to align with how learning actually happens.

Process-based curriculum recognizes learning as an interaction between the teacher and the student, with learning happening in both directions (Stenhouse, 1975). The focus is more on big ideas where the curriculum *is* the interaction, allowing for a more organic learning experience. This has the practical benefit of having less "stuff" to assess, and when implemented correctly, allows greater flexibility on how that interaction is taught and learned, allowing freedom for student input into the curriculum.

We have to be careful here, though. More than likely the state you work in and/or the school system in which you teach has some pretty specific ideas about what your students should be learning. Within the confines of formal schooling, there is only so much leverage the student has in negotiating learning goals, if any. The NGSS has defined performance expectations that you will have to assess, no matter how many great arguments your students make. There is a great deal of flexibility, but there is also a definite structure.

This is why I advocate a hybrid approach to curriculum development, where we are systematic about our goals and the process we go through to develop activities, but we leave open the ability to re-evaluate our own teaching and curriculum decisions based on feedback from students. We have a well-defined plan, but we recognize the need for occasional flexibility. For example, we may have a performance expectation well defined from the NGSS, but we have a great deal of flexibility in how we build a learning progression that gets everyone there, and we have the freedom to go beyond strictly delineated products in the design of that progression.

Figure 3.1 shows a schematic diagram of the hybrid curriculum development process. It looks like a funnel, because we get more and more detail and more and more specific as we move down the list. For this book, we use the USA-based NGSS as our set of broad-based learning goals and learn to build a curriculum off of these goals using this hybrid

Figure 3.1 Schematic diagram of a hybrid product/process approach to curriculum development using the NGSS as a guide to defining learning goals. Locations where we find science thinking within curriculum are highlighted

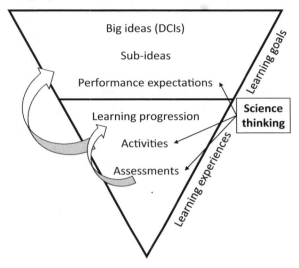

Source: Based on the process detailed in Moore, 2017

approach. However, the principles are generative and can work with most any set of standards.

We start out with the big ideas, break these into smaller sub-ideas, and develop broad performance expectations from these sub-ideas. This sets up our set of learning goals. Then, we decide on a learning progression that could lead a student towards understanding demonstrated by the performance expectation. We create specific activities within that progression, and then we assess performance in those activities. All of these items form the overall learning experience for the student. The arrows in the figure represent "re-evaluation." Occasionally, we learn during assessment that the activities failed miserably to foster understanding, or that the learning progression was missing pieces. In some cases, assessment can lead us to develop completely new goals.

For those of us teaching in the context of well-defined standards such as the NGSS (or the Nebraska College and Career Ready Science Standards, in my particular case), the first part of the process is done for us. The NGSS have a clearly laid out set of performance expectations for each grade level and disciplinary area. The complicated part, the part you the teacher are now responsible for, is developing the learning experiences and assessments that build students up to these performance expectations. Doing this successfully requires deep discipline-based understanding on the part of the teacher in combination with knowledge and practice in science education methods. This integration of content with content-specific pedagogy we call Pedagogical Content Knowledge (PCK) (Ball & McDiarmid, 1990; Shulman, 1987). You need to know where the student is starting with respect to content (and doing/thinking!), where you want them to go, what it takes to get them there, what concepts they need to build an understanding, and how to assess whether or not they are progressing. Easy stuff, right?

Unfortunately, this is too small a book to go into great detail on PCK in all sub-disciplines, or even one. I also have no real expertise myself on PCK in biology, as one example. In Part III of this book, I will go through a detailed example from middle school physical science to show you how we use PCK and the product/process hybrid approach to build a learning progression. The principles are generative, so you should still be able to extract a framework for using your own knowledge and years of experience to do the same in your domain.

For now, I'm going to assume you have a pretty good understanding of your domain and your students' initial approach. Many of you reading this have more classroom experience than me, so you don't really need my help in this area. Instead, we're going to focus on how to incorporate science thinking into those learning progressions and how to execute the *explicit-reflective-count* framework in your classroom. We'll see an example of how all the pieces fit together into a full progression in the final chapter.

Incorporating Science Thinking into Curriculum

Let's revisit Figure 3.1 to see where we can find the science thinking patterns we listed in Chapter 1. As discussed in Chapter 2, we find science thinking littered throughout the performance expectations of the NGSS, even when they aren't explicit. Therefore, science thinking and the minimum set of six patterns we have already identified are components of our learning goals. Since thinking is ultimately something we do in the moment, we don't necessarily include the thinking patterns within our development of a learning progression. However, when students are in action, those thinking abilities will be on full display. It is at the activity and assessment levels that we need to build in explicit instruction on science thinking, reflective discussions, and formative and summative tests of thinking ability.

We've discussed what activities should look like: cognitive apprenticeship. I will spend Part II of this book showing you explicit examples of using cognitive apprenticeship and the *explicit-reflective-count* framework. We still need to discuss how we will go about assessing science thinking.

Thinking is a verb, as opposed to learned content, so our approach to assessing thinking can and should be different from our traditional approach to assessing content knowledge alone. Standardized tests typically focus on the student's proficiency in recalling learned facts, and can be a fairly efficient way of measuring learned content knowledge. However, how effective would a similar assessment be at measuring thinking?

It actually goes deeper than just assessing thinking, though, due to the tight integration between knowing, doing, and thinking necessary for understanding. In the first chapter, we discussed situated cognition as an action-based model for how students learn. Students can only "understand" science ideas if they understand how the practice of science leads to those ideas. With respect to content, that means that we should not only assess the student's thinking abilities, but we should assess content knowledge within the context of practice, too. We have to do it all at the same time!

The types of activities students do when practicing science are multifaceted and open-ended. This makes assessment design for practices more difficult. Scoring rubrics, however, can provide the flexibility such activity requires while also maintaining a structure on which students can base learning. Rubric design experts Dannielle Stevens and Antonia Levi describe the scoring rubric as follows (Stevens & Levi, 2005):

> At its most basic, a rubric is a scoring tool that lays out the specific expectations for an assignment. Rubrics divide an assignment into its component parts and provide a detailed description of what constitutes acceptable or unacceptable levels of performance for each of those parts.

There are entire books and websites on designing good rubrics. In particular, I refer you to the University of Colorado Denver's excellent online rubric writing tutorial or Stevens's and Levi's book, both of which are listed in the references (The Center for Faculty Development, University of Colorado Denver, 2006; Stevens & Levi, 2005). Educational consultant Charlotte Danielson has an excellent series of books on rubric design and performance tasks for mathematics published by Routledge Eye on Education that can provide insight to your science lessons (Danielson & Hansen, 2016; Danielson & Dragoon, 2016; Danielson & Marquez, 2016). However, how can we incorporate the generic lessons on rubric design into a system from creating rubrics that assess student work in science thinking *and* practice *and* content all at the same time?

Table 3.4 shows the basic steps to rubric design for integrated knowing, doing, and thinking that I discuss in greater detail elsewhere (Moore, 2017). These steps are based on the research on rubrics and general assessment, specifically tailored to our needs with respect to the NGSS and the *Framework* (Stevens & Levi, 2005). First, we determine the learning goal for the activity. Then, we define the evidence statements to look for in student work. We define individual criterions based on the content of interest. For each criterion, we design a rating scale and write descriptions of expectations for each criterion. Finally, we deploy the rubric and re-evaluate everything based on student feedback and results.

We have already discussed the first step, determining the learning goal. For the second step, each of the performance expectations laid out in the NGSS comes with an associated set of *evidence statements*. Evidence statements describe what you can look for in student work to provide evidence of understanding. These evidence statements are very useful, since they can serve as the foundation for our assessment rubrics. Table 3.5 shows the basic evidence statements you would look for with respect to the following example performance expectation:

MS-PS2–5. Conduct an investigation and evaluate the experimental design to provide evidence that fields exist between objects exerting forces on each other even though the objects are not in contact.

TABLE 3.4 STEPS TO CREATING A RUBRIC THAT ASSESSES SCIENCE PRACTICE IN CONTEXT (MOORE, 2017)

Step	Description
1	Determine the learning goal for the activity
2	Define the evidence statements to look for in student work
3	Define individual criterions based on the content
4	Design a rating scale, with descriptions of expectations for each criterion
5	Re-evaluate the rubric

TABLE 3.5 EVIDENCE STATEMENTS FOR CONDUCTING AN INVESTIGATION AND EVALUATING DESIGN

The student ...	
1	identifies the phenomenon to be investigated
2	identifies evidence to address the purpose of the investigation
3	plans the investigation
4	collects the data
5	evaluates the design

Source: Adapted from NGSS Lead States, 2013

When assessing a student's work conducting an investigation and evaluating the experimental design, we're looking for five pieces of evidence:

The student:

1. identifies the phenomenon being investigated
2. identifies the purpose of the investigation
3. plans the investigation
4. collects and records the data
5. evaluates the design.

These evidence statements are general for all of the performance expectations dealing with the science practice of conducting investigations. The specific context will change with varying DCIs. Evidence statements for all of the performance expectations can be found on the website for the NGSS (nextgenscience.org), and can serve as the foundation for assessment rubrics that you can use both for formative and summative assessment (NGSS Lead States, 2013).

Where exactly does science thinking fit into these evidence statements, though? Let's go back and think about the tangled web of practices, cross-cutting concepts, and science thinking patterns detailed in Figure 2.2. We can break down the specific practices into well-defined activities, because ultimately practice is activity. As I discuss in previous work, the practices themselves do have fuzzy borders, but there is some clear delineation (Moore, 2017). Within the execution of practices, though, thinking can be done with multiple patterns manifesting in the mind during any individual practice.

To illustrate this idea, and how the science thinking patterns weave into the evidence statements for a specific practice (in this case, conducting an investigation), look at Figure 3.2. As an example, when we are evaluating how a student plans the investigation (evidence of practice), we must also look to make sure they are using appropriate control of variables (evidence of thinking). Other types of thinking can come into play, as well, so you have flexibility on what it is you ultimately want to evaluate and make explicit during a certain activity.

Example 3.1 shows a partial rubric based on the NGSS evidence statements for an activity completed based on performance expectation MS-PS2–5. In this particular example, we are only looking at evidence statement #3 "plans the investigation" from Table 3.5. The overall layout of the rubric at the top-level is generic across all activities where the student would conduct and evaluate an investigation, with the evidence statements used as our top-level criteria. At the lower-level, the rubric is specific for the individual activity or activities, in this case, for an investigation that produces evidence of fields.

Figure 3.2 Sketch showing how science thinking patterns are woven into the NGSS evidence statements

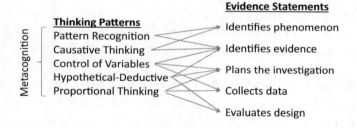

Example 3.1 Partial rubric for conducting and evaluating an investigation on magnetic fields

Plans the investigation			
	Unsatisfactory	**Needs improvement**	**Satisfactory**
Describes how the magnetic field will be measured with the available equipment	The student does not describe how the magnetic field will be measured.	The student describes how the magnetic field will be measured, but the measurement either can't be done with the materials provided, or will not result in measuring the magnetic field.	The student describes how the magnetic field will be measured and it will result in a useful measurement.

(Continued)

Example 3.1 (Continued)

Plans the investigation			
	Unsatisfactory	**Needs improvement**	**Satisfactory**
The plan *identifies the relevant variables*	Only one or no relevant variables are identified	Most but not all relevant variables are identified.	All relevant variables are identified.
Appropriate *isolation of variables* is incorporated in the plan	Appropriate isolation of variables is not incorporated in the plan.	Variables are isolated, but the specific independent and dependent variable pairs are not explicitly identified.	Specific independent and dependent variables are identified with appropriate isolation such that a pattern can be determined.

In Example 3.1, I have underlined the specific language dealing with the science thinking patterns we are looking to assess. In the performance of the practice of planning an investigation, the student must also be able to demonstrate acceptable control of variables. As described in Chapter 1, control of variables has two components:

1. the recognition of relevant variables, and
2. the ability to isolate and control those variables in experiments.

In the partial rubric shown in Example 3.1, we have individual criterion for each component of the control of variables science thinking pattern.

Next, we define the rating scale (Step 4 from Table 3.4). Notice that for each evidence statement and sub-criterion in Example 3.1, the student can achieve a score of either unsatisfactory, needs improvement, or satisfactory. This is where the final re-evaluation step (Step 5) will be necessary to hone your rubric with time and experience. It is usually fairly easy to know what we *want* from the student. It is more difficult to anticipate what the student will actually do. That makes successful rubric building an iterative process, since there are many available paths to the student. As you begin to assess students, you will start to see what little aspects they need to improve on their way towards the goal. This will allow you to do two things:

1. design better, more detailed rubrics for future use, and
2. make changes to the learning experience that can lead to the improvement you seek.

Again, that's the evaluative step in curriculum development that's key if you want to involve the student and their feedback into the learning process (and also Step 5 in rubric writing).

You should think of the rubric as a guide *for the student*, as opposed to merely an assessment instrument. In fact, you will want to give your students any rubric you will use to assess an assignment *before* they are tasked with the assignment, including tests. This makes your descriptions of expectations a key learning tool for the student, serving as a learning guide they can use during their performance. This also satisfies the "make it explicit" component of our framework. The clearer your descriptions of your expectations are, the easier it will be for the student to meet those expectations. Also, it's critically important that the same types of rubrics used for low-stakes formative assessment are also used when it comes time to test students. To quote assessment specialist Rick Stiggins, "students can hit any target that they know about and that holds still for them" (Stiggins & Chappuis, 2017). It is unfair of you to move the target!

In the following chapters, I will provide more details on rubric-based assessment of science thinking as we look at some specific classroom activities. It is also possible to incorporate multiple-choice based assessment with science thinking, ideally as a quick in-the-moment formative assessment. I'll show you some examples of this, as well, as we progress through Part II of the book.

Summary

In summary, students can only understand science by knowing, doing, and thinking in the science classroom. A shift in focus from traditional descriptive content knowledge towards an integration of knowing, doing, and thinking requires a similar shift in pedagogy. In this chapter, we have synthesized the research literature on effective teaching for practice and cognitive improvement. Specifically, we learned that *apprenticeship* is a model for teaching science thinking that is effective when done well. Inquiry-based approaches to teaching science work when *all* of the components of apprenticeship are included. The most important and most overlooked components center around metacognition, such as explicit focus on thinking, student reflection on their own thinking, and strong mechanisms for making good thinking count towards the grades students receive.

The biggest takeaway from this chapter was that you absolutely must make science thinking count in your classroom if you want your students to take science thinking seriously. To that end, we discussed the hybrid product/process approach to developing curriculum, and we introduced methods for building thinking-based criteria into scoring rubrics. This short introduction to teaching theory, curriculum development, and assessment has prepared you for the classroom-tested lessons we'll discuss in the next section of this book.

The following is a brief summary of the main points:

◆ Getting students actively constructing their own knowledge leads to greater content knowledge learning and retention, but metacognition is essential to improving abilities in practice and thinking.

◆ The principle methods of cognitive apprenticeship are as follows:

   ◇ modeling
   ◇ coaching
   ◇ scaffolding
   ◇ reflection
   ◇ articulation
   ◇ exploration.

◆ Well-designed inquiry-based methods and activities are proven to improve student learning and are fun and enjoyable for the student. However, it's not enough for students to physically participate in the activities, they must also mentally participate.

◆ This requires you to do the following during the activities:

   ◇ *Be explicit* about the practice and thinking needed for the activity.
   ◇ *Be reflective* about those practices and thinking both during and after the activity.
   ◇ *Make it count* by clearly and consistently assessing practices and thinking.

◆ When making it count, it must be clear to the student that the practice and thinking are at least equally as important as the content.

◆ Assessment must be built into curriculum design. You can't have one without the other.

◆ Curriculum is best thought of as a process, as opposed to a series of products.

◆ NGSS performance expectations can be used to define learning goals.

◆ In designing a learning progression that achieves our learning goals, we must go beyond the NGSS. Just because science thinking isn't explicitly in the NGSS doesn't mean we can't use it in our classes. In fact, we must!

◆ NGSS evidence statements provide a useful foundation for writing criteria in rubrics.

◆ Good rubrics are consistent in their top-level approach with respect to practices, with individual criterion requiring specific content knowledge and thinking patterns. Therefore, good rubrics combine the assessment of knowing, doing, and thinking *at the same time*.

References

Bachtold, M. (2013). What do students "construct" according to constructivism in science education? *Research in Science Education, 43,* 2477–2496.

Banchi, H., & Bell, R. (2008). The many levels of inquiry. *Science and Children,* 26–29.

Barab, S., & Hay, K. (2001). Doing science at the elbows of experts: Issues related to the science apprenticeship camp. *Journal of Research in Science Teaching, 38*(1), 70–102.

Blank, L. M. (2000). A metacognitive learning cycle: A better warranty for student understanding? *Science Education, 84*(4), 486–506.

Brown, J., Collins, A., & Duguid, P. (1989). Situated Cognition and the Culture of Learning. *Educational Researcher, 18,* 32.

Cornbleth, C. (1990). *Curriculum in Context.* Basingstoke: Falmer Press.

Danielson, C., & Dragoon, J. (2016). *Performance Tasks and Rubrics for Upper Elementary Mathematics* (2nd ed.). New York: Routledge.

Danielson, C., & Hansen, P. (2016). *Performance Tasks and Rubrics for Early Elementary Mathematics* 2nd ed. New York: Routledge.

Danielson, C., & Marquez, E. (2016). *Performance Tasks and Rubrics for Middle School Mathematics* 2nd ed. New York: Routledge.

Edmondson, K. M., & Novak, J. D. (1993). The interplay of scientific epistemological views, learning strategies, and attitudes of college students. *Journal of Research in Science Teaching, 30,* 547–559.

Etkina, E., & Mestre, J. P. (2004). Implications of Learning Research for Teaching Science to Non-Science Majors. *SENCER*, (pp. 1–26). Harrisburg, PA.

Ghefaili, A. (2003). Cognitive apprenticeship, technology, and the contextualization of learning environments. *Journal of Educational Computing, Design, and Online Learning, 4.*

Kuhn, D. (2004). What is scientific thinking and how does it develop? In U. Goswami (ed.), *Blackwell Handbook of Childhood Cognitive Development* (pp. 371–393). Malden, MA, USA: Wiley-Blackwell.

Lawson, A. E. (2000). The generality of hypothetico-deductive reasoning: Making scientific thinking explicit. *American Biology Teacher, 62*, 482.

Moore, C. (2017). *Creating Scientists: Teaching and Assessing Science Practice for the NGSS.* New York, NY: Routledge.

Moore, J. C. (2012). Transitional to Formal Operational: Using Authentic Research Experiences to Get Non-Science Students to Think More Like Scientists. *European Journal of Physics Education, 3*(4), 1–12.

Moore, J. C., & Rubbo, L. J. (2012). Scientific reasoning abilities of nonscience majors in physics-based courses. *Physical Review Special Topics – Physics Education Research, 8*, 010106.

NGSS Lead States. (2013). *Evidence Statements.* Retrieved from Next Generation Science Standards: www.nextgenscience.org

Papert, S. (1991). Situating constructionism. In I. Harel, & S. Papert (eds), *Constructionism: Research Reports and Essays* (pp. 1–11). Norwood, NJ: Ablex.

Pratt, D. (1998). *Five Perspectives on Teaching in Adult and Higher Education.* Malabar, FL: Krieger Publishing Company.

Reif, F., & Larkin, J. (1991). Cognition in scientific and everyday domains: Comparisons and learning implications. *Journal of Research in Science Teaching, 28*, 733–760.

Roth, W.-M., & Jornet, A. (2013). Toward a theory of experience. *Science Education, 98*(1), 106–126.

Smith, M. K. (2000). *Curriculum theory and practice.* Retrieved from *The Encyclopedia of Informal Education*: www.infed.org/biblio/b-curric.htm

Stenhouse, L. (1975). *An Introduction to Curriculum Research and Development.* London: Heinemann.

Stevens, D. D., & Levi, A. J. (2005). *An Introduction to Rubrics.* Sterling, VA: Stylus.

Stiggins, R., & Chappuis, J. (2017). *Introduction to Student-Involved Assessment FOR Learning* 7th ed. New York: Pearson.

Taba, H. (1962). *Curriculum Development: Theory and Practice.* New York: Harcourt Brace and World.

The Center for Faculty Development, University of Colorado Denver. (2006). Retrieved from Creating a Rubric: An Online Tutorial for Faculty: www.ucdenver.edu/faculty_staff/faculty/center-for-faculty-development/Documents/Tutorials/Rubrics/index.htm

Tyler, R. W. (1949). *Basic Principles of Curriculum and Instruction.* Chicago: University of Chicago Press.

White, B. Y., & Frederiksen, J. R. (1998). Inquiry, Modeling, and Metacognition: Making Science Accessible to All Students. *Cognition and Instruction, 16*(1), 3–118.

Part II
Science Thinking In the Classroom

4

Recognizing Patterns and Making Connections

"Creativity and insight almost always involve an experience of acute pattern recognition: the eureka moment in which we perceive the interconnection between disparate concepts or ideas to reveal something new."

—Jason Silva (Silva, 2011)

Pattern recognition is not only the foundation of science, but arguably the foundation of human thought (Mattson, 2014). The modern practice of science only works because nature keeps repeating itself, and we only really trust science findings because this repetition results in the possibility for predictions that we can test again and again. The scientist's job is to discover these repeating patterns, observe how they repeat, determine why they repeat, and use models of the patterns to make new predictions. Therefore, the student of science needs the thinking abilities to recognize and observe patterns. These patterns can manifest as repeating forms, such as shapes and colors of specific fish species, or repeating events, such as seasons or solar eclipses. Pattern thinking goes beyond simple recognition, though. Good science thinking requires the ability to use patterns to organize and classify content, as well as prompt questions about the relationships and/or variables that might influence the pattern.

This chapter focuses on what psychologists and cognitive scientists think goes on in our mind with respect to pattern recognition, and how we can use this understanding to inform our teaching. Our goal is to improve pattern recognition abilities, and we will do this by explicitly naming them, getting students to think about what their minds are doing in the process, and looking at strategies for assessing students' thinking with respect to patterns.

Specifically, we will discuss three basic theories on how we perceive patterns, and then see how these three theories can be applied within the context of scientific thinking. We'll use these ideas and the *explicit-reflective-count* framework from the previous chapter to inform a practical "Thinking Task" worksheet that you can incorporate into any lesson where pattern recognition is used. Finally, I'll show you several activities that involve pattern recognition and discuss how the thinking task can be easily built into the lessons. We'll progress from qualitative patterns of repeating forms to quantitative patterns of mathematical functions, and eventually learn how students can begin to build their own predictive models and/or hypotheses from observed patterns in data.

Pattern Recognition in Childhood

In psychologist Jean Piaget's theory of cognitive development, the abstract principles of thinking called "seriation" and "oddity" usually begin to develop before children attend grade school at around the age of four (Inhelder & Piaget, 1969). Seriation is the ability to arrange items in a logical order, while oddity is the ability to choose items from a group that differ from others in the group. Both focus on separation and/or distinction due to quantitative dimension such as length, weight, etc. Seriation requires the understanding that objects can be ordered, and oddity requires the understanding that objects can be distinguished. This forms the concrete foundation of what we might consider formal pattern recognition, and it typically begins to happen in pre-school, at least with concrete, observable objects.

As we begin our discussion on teaching pattern recognition, knowing how seriation ability develops through childhood is important, since although the child may begin to seriate before formal schooling, the development of the ability is gradual. Piaget and Alina Szeminska found that there were three distinct stages of ability development, where children could not arrange ten different-length rods in order without significant trial and error until around 7 to 8 years of age (Piaget & Szeminska, 1941).

This means that concrete pattern recognition and differentiation are developing during elementary school, which makes the incorporation of instruction in pattern thinking critical as children learn about science during K–6 levels. This also means that we must be careful to match the sophistication and types of pattern recognition we can expect to what is reasonable with respect to the typical child's cognitive development.

Why is pattern recognition important, even at such a young age? I chose this particular thinking pattern as the first in our set for a reason. It could be argued that pattern recognition is a foundational ability, where many other tasks become easier for the student after they have improved with this ability. There is a mountain of evidence that shows developing strong abilities in seriation and patterning helps in the development of all-around problem-solving skills and other cognitive tasks, including content learning and retention. For example, a research group at George Mason University found that focusing on seriation and oddity in an early-childhood Head Start program resulted in improved cognitive skills compared to a focus on letters, numbers, and art (Kidd, et al., 2012). In fact, the team found that the seriation/oddity group performed better at learning letters and word sounds than the group that specifically focused on letters and words! Therefore, the development of pattern recognition helps far beyond the context of science. Science lessons in elementary school are actually excellent opportunities to focus on pattern recognition, which can carry over into improved performance in seemingly different contexts.

My own research group has seen a similar trend among post-secondary students at the opposite end of formal schooling, so its importance carries throughout the grade levels. Although we didn't look at pattern recognition specifically, we did find that broadly measured scientific reasoning ability, which includes pattern recognition, was correlated to a student's "learning potential." Gains in content knowledge were strongly correlated with science thinking ability (Moore & Rubbo, 2012). Furthermore, we observed what we have called a "threshold effect," where students struggled to apply an appropriate framing in a problem-solving task until they reached a certain level of thinking ability (Moore & Slisko, 2017). This is not terribly surprising when considering our *knowing-doing-thinking* model for understanding.

How Do We Perceive Patterns

So pattern recognition is important. But what exactly is pattern recognition and how does it go beyond simple seriation? What exactly happens in our minds as we think about patterns or perform patterning tasks? The simple, honest answer to these questions is: we don't know! The less simple (but still honest) answer is that our understanding of the psychology and cognitive science underlying pattern recognition is complicated and fraught with debate. Furthermore, our theories on pattern recognition are all relatively new, with most of the modeling work being done within the past decade and motivated by machine learning. I'm going to discuss three basic theories of pattern recognition, but understand that they each have their problems from a psychological/cognitive perspective. However, they do serve as a good foundation for building a *practical* approach to teaching pattern recognition.

Table 4.1 shows the three basic theories of pattern recognition with short descriptions. *Template matching theory* assumes every perceived object is stored as a "template" into long-term memory. *Prototype matching theory* compares incoming sensory input to an average prototype developed during exposure to related stimuli. *Feature matching theory* assumes that we try to match common features of the stimuli with features stored in memory.

In template matching theory, the stimuli we perceive from objects that we see or interact with gets stored as a template into long-term memory (Eysenck & Keane, 2003; Shugen, 2002). Any new, incoming information gets compared to these templates, where we either find an exact match, or create a new template. This theory definitely has some limitations. For example, we can easily identify that A, *A*, and **A** all represent the same letter, as opposed to completely different templates, and I could change the font to one you've never seen before and you can still make the correct identification. I could also draw a sketch of a car. You could look at my

TABLE 4.1 PATTERN RECOGNITION THEORIES

Theory	Description
Template Matching	Incoming stimuli are matched one-to-one with templates stored in long-term memory. If the stimuli don't match a remembered template exactly, a new template is created.
Prototype Matching	Incoming stimuli are matched to prototypes stored in long-term memory. These prototypes are averages of many other perceived patterns. The new perception doesn't have to exactly match the prototype in order for recognition to occur, so long as there are shared features.
Feature Matching	Incoming stimuli are filtered through feature detectors in the nervous system. Feature detectors are assumed to be biological, such as groups of neurons. These detectors encode specific perceptual features on the incoming stimuli. When features repeat, we are able to identify patterns.

horrible sketch and more than likely still be able to identify it as a car, even though it would be something you've never seen. Template matching theory also suggests that we would be storing a nearly infinite number of templates at an early age, which seems like an improbable cognitive load.

Prototype matching theory eschews the exact one-to-one matching found in template matching and instead suggests that we build a sort of "prototype" of sensory input based on shared features. The prototype is an average of many other perceived patterns, where the new perception doesn't have to exactly match the prototype in order for recognition to occur, so long as there are shared features. My sketch of the car might show a side-view with two wheels and a hump in the middle. You can compare the sketch to the prototype of a car found in your mind, which shares the features you see in my sketch. You can also recognize that my sketch is of a car, as opposed to a bus, since your bus prototype has a boxier shape with a different length-to-width ratio. This theory has the benefit of reducing the number of stored templates by standardizing them into a single representation. However, some objects cannot necessarily be "averaged" into a single prototype. A common example found in cognitive psychology textbooks involves various forms of canines (Eysenck & Keane, 2003). Even though dogs, wolves, and foxes share similar features, they are not all the same. You'd probably still be able to distinguish a fox from a small dog, though.

Feature matching theory assumes that part of our pattern recognition ability is biological, or based on our brain hardware. Any incoming stimuli are filtered by specific detectors in our brain, which are composed of groups of neurons. One set of feature filters might detect edges, where there is a strong contrast between light and dark, for example. As perceptual information flows through the nervous system, more complex feature detectors respond to more complex and stimuli specific aspects of the information. These more complex filters may be developed with age and experience through complex neuron structures built as we process and make sense of more and more information. As you perceive my car sketch, you might first sense the rectangular white paper using edge detectors in your brain. Then, the stark contrast between the inked lines and white paper is filtered by a more complex grouping of neurons. This is matched with past experiences of this set of features to recognize the item as a sketch and not a photograph. Finally, your brain may begin to filter the shapes, and ultimately match this specific series of shapes to past stimuli resulting in identification of the item as a sketch of a car.

As I mentioned, all of these basic theories have some drawbacks, specifically with respect to our ability to utilize surrounding context surprisingly well. For eaxlpme, yuor ailibty to raed tihs stencene. However, we can still extract some practical use from such a basic understanding of pattern recognition for use in your classroom. Notice that prototyping requires some sort of feature detection system. In reality, both processes are probably happening within our brains, where stimuli are filtered based on features, and then prototypes are built based on repetition of those features in certain ways.

Thinking Task: Pattern Recognition

It is not within the scope of this book to argue for or against any specific pattern recognition theory, nor is it within my skill set to do so. However, we can use aspects of each theory to inform an approach to getting students to think about what it is they are doing when completing patterning tasks. We learned in Chapter 3 that student metacognition is *the* key to improvements in deployment of science thinking. We must get them to actively think about what they are thinking when engaged in science practice. To do this with respect to pattern recognition, we can utilize the foundational pieces of each theory to inform questions that we can ask the student to ponder.

Ultimately, we can break down patterning into three key components: templates, prototypes, and features. To frame an experience within a template model, we might wonder where we have seen this type of stimuli before. Within a prototype framing we might compare the experience to some other experience from our past. Finally, we could break down an experience into smaller, more general features to think about it from a feature framing. The combination of all three allows the mind to make connections between what is observed, what is known, and what is being done.

Thinking Task 4.1 shows a short series of questions that we can insert into any lesson that includes patterning. This can be done as either a separate worksheet, the questions could be inserted into an existing worksheet, or you could simply ask these questions during the completion of the activity. As you will see in the example activities later in this chapter, you can also edit these questions to better fit your specific content. Either way, the question set serves as a metacognitive activity that forces reflection on pattern recognition.

Thinking Task 4.1 Pattern Recognition

Where have you seen this behavior before?
   What does this behavior compare to?
   What features of this behavior are relevant and what other behavior has these features?

The questions are informed by the three pattern matching theories we just discussed. The following lists each specific pattern matching theory together with the reflective question that was motivated by the theory:

   Template matching – where have you seen this before?
      Prototype matching – what does this compare to?
      Feature matching – what features are relevant and what else has these features?

The three basic principles we learned in the previous chapter for teaching science thinking were to be explicit, be reflective, and make thinking count. In the implementation of the pattern recognition thinking task, it is important to be explicit with what you are doing. You can do this through text like you see bolded at the top of Thinking Task 4.1, or orally by consistently highlighting to students that what they are doing now is pattern recognition. By asking the three questions in Thinking Task 4.1, we are forcing the student to be reflective about what was going on in their minds. You can do this formally through a worksheet with written responses, or informally through a class discussion. Finally, we will discuss how to make it count by looking at assessment for some of the example activities in the rest of this chapter.

Multiple Representations: Building Circuits

Let's think a little deeper about templates, prototypes, and features. The example I used above was that the slight stylistic changes between A, *A*, and **A** didn't change our fundamental understanding and recognition of the letter. However, as content becomes more complex, seemingly similar ways of expressing the same idea are not necessarily obvious (Larkin & Simon, 1987). For example, research in physics education has shown that the symbols in mathematical equations and the relations between the symbols have very little meaning to students (Larkin, 1985). They can manipulate the equations, but they don't understand what the variables really mean and how they relate to other variables. This is fundamentally a failure at patterning, where the student doesn't connect the mathematical representation of physical behavior (the variables and equation) with other representations, such as graphs, pictures, videos, or even live unfolding events. They either don't form prototypes that include mathematical representations, or they can't connect the features common between the math and the other representations.

This isn't necessarily the fault of the students, since traditional physics instruction, as one example, rarely focuses explicitly on this type of pattern formation. As we keep encountering, explicit instruction and metacognition on thinking patterns is critical if they are to develop. As teachers, we can provide the structure necessary to improve connection-making by having students represent physical processes in multiple ways and convert back and forth from one representation to another (Chi, et al., 1981). By being explicit about this process, you can help your students make connections between concrete ways of representing something such as pictures, and abstract representations such as graphs and/or equations.

Let's look at electric circuits for one example of switching between representations that doesn't use mathematics, and is therefore more appropriate across grade levels. We're going to look at an activity that helps students learn to switch back and forth between pictorial representations of electric circuits, abstract schematic representations, and then actual physical circuits that they build.

Activity 4.1 shows a series of short activities on circuits adapted from the book *Physics by Inquiry* (McDermott, 1996). Students start with pictorial representations of the realistic circuits, learn abstract schematic representations and how they connect to the pictorial and real components, and then practice switching back and forth, culminating in the ability to build a physical circuit using a schematic representation.

Activity 4.1   Using Models to Describe Electric Circuits

Part I: Recreating a Circuit from Pictures (Modeling)

Figure 4.1 shows a realistic drawing of an electric circuit. The instructor will model the thinking process used to build a real circuit that matches the drawing.

Figure 4.1 Drawing of a circuit

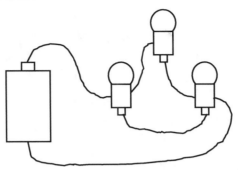

Figure 4.2 The same circuit with its standard schematic representation

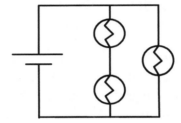

Pattern Recognition:

What features of the picture are relevant and how do they relate to the physical circuit?

Part II: Schematics

Figure 4.2 shows the circuit pictorially represented in Figure 4.1 along with what we call a schematic representation of the same circuit.

Pattern Recognition:

Which schematic symbol represents the battery, and why do you think so?

Which schematic symbol represents a bulb, and why do you think so?

Which schematic symbol represents a wire, and why do you think so?

Where else have you seen the use of a something like a "schematic" diagram?

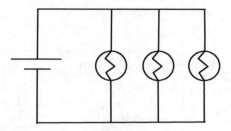

Figure 4.3 Schematic representation of another circuit

Part III: Building Circuits from Schematics

Figure 4.3 shows a schematic for another circuit.

Draw a picture of what the circuit would look like in real life. Then, using the materials provided, build the circuit.

In Part I, the instructor would model the thinking process necessary to go from a picture to a real circuit. Specifically, it is important to highlight how the lines represent wires, the rectangle is a battery with the little hump signifying its direction, and the bulb parts, such as the two metal connections on the bulb bottom match the real pieces of a real bulb. In my own modeling of circuit construction, I focus on going from one side of the battery to the other, and adding pieces to the physical circuit as I go. At the end of Part I, we want the student to think about specific features of the representation, so that they can begin to prototype. Notice how a question from Thinking Task 4.1 was re-written to fit within the context.

In Part II, the student evaluates the differences and similarities between a picture representation and a more abstract and formal schematic representation. Here again, the student is recognizing what shared features the two have, and in the process constructing content knowledge about schematic symbols by using pattern recognition. These first two activities serve to create a more abstract prototype of an electric circuit in the student's mind that they can utilize in the future for more complex circuit tasks. We also have the student explicitly think about other types of representations they may have seen in the past that are similar to schematics, such as blueprints or maps.

Finally, in Part III the student uses the framework they have constructed in their mind to go from one representation to another. We could extend this activity by showing the student a completely different real-life circuit and then having them draw a schematic diagram for it.

Often times, this representation-switching is an implied ability, where we as instructors just assume that students will be able to do it with little difficulty. However, this is very rarely the case. My own research group has observed difficulties with what seems like the simple task of building a circuit from a schematic while working with adult middle school teachers. In most physical science classes, teachers often just start with the schematics without thinking about making connections between what the students are physically doing with what they're showing.

Leaving important connections implicit is understandable from the adult, highly educated professional perspective. As a materials scientist, I spent years developing electronic devices with electrical engineers, so these types of representations are natural to me due to constant exposure and pattern recognition through time. After teaching science for decades, you've probably built similar experiences, so it's easy for you to forget the struggle you had with making these connections yourself. However, your 4th grader has had no similar experience and their pattern recognition abilities are still growing.

Metacognitive tasks such as this simple example make the thinking explicit, and allow your students the time to make important connections. It also highlights to the student the underlying importance of the thinking itself. We're often in a rush to move through content, but it's important to take the time to make connections between different ways of expressing ideas, so that the more complex situations eventually become equivalent to recognizing the connection between A, *A*, and **A**.

Taxonomies: Magnets

So far, we've focused on pattern recognition necessary for learning in science, but not necessarily the more obvious types of pattern recognition used in the practice of science. In the following sections, we'll look at some example activities where we combine knowing, doing, and thinking. These activities are all fundamentally based on pattern recognition as used in the sciences, with a collection of different science practices and content. I will show you how to weave the questions in Thinking Task 4.1 into your lessons to make pattern recognition explicit and force reflection.

Let's begin by looking at an example where we start the process of developing explicit pattern recognition, in which a student is taught to recognize common features and then use those features to group things like a scientist would. The following example discusses an activity where students build a *taxonomy*.

In Activity 4.2, students are given a set of small cylinders all of the same length and diameter. The cylinders are made up of different materials, such as wood, brass, aluminum, plastic, iron, and two unmarked magnets. The task is to group the cylinders based on their interactions with each other.

Activity 4.2 Developing a Taxonomy of Materials Based on Magnetic Interaction

Science Practice:

Developing and using models

You have been provided with a set of cylinders, each having the same length and diameter. The materials which the cylinders are made of are not necessarily the same.

Arrange the cylinders into at least three different classes based on their *interactions* with each other. Test other objects you have, such as coins, pencils, parts of the table, etc. and put them into your classes.

How many types of interactions did you observe? Describe them.
Pattern Recognition:

Where have you seen this behavior before?
What features of the materials were relevant to their classification?
Did it matter whether or not they were metal? Why or why not?
This type of grouping activity is common across different fields of science. Describe an experience where you have done this type of grouping before. How was that experience similar, and how was it different?

This activity could be used as the beginning of a learning progression leading up to a specific performance expectation in the NGSS. For example, in the 3rd grade magnetic interactions are discussed, as evidenced by the following performance expectation, with increasing sophistication on the topic building through middle and high school (NGSS Lead States, 2013):

> 3-PS2–3. Ask questions to determine cause and effect relationships of electric or magnetic interactions between two objects not in contact with each other.

Students ask questions about magnetic force between two permanent magnets, and/or the force between a magnet and paperclips, and/or the strength of the force exerted by one magnet versus two magnets stacked together. We'll go into more depth about developing a full learning progression of magentic interactions for elementary and middle school physical science in the last chapter of this book when we put all of the pieces together.

For now, Figure 4.4 shows an example of student work completing Activity 4.2. The student can be seen recognizing the three types of

Figure 4.4 Example of student work sorting cylinders based on interactions

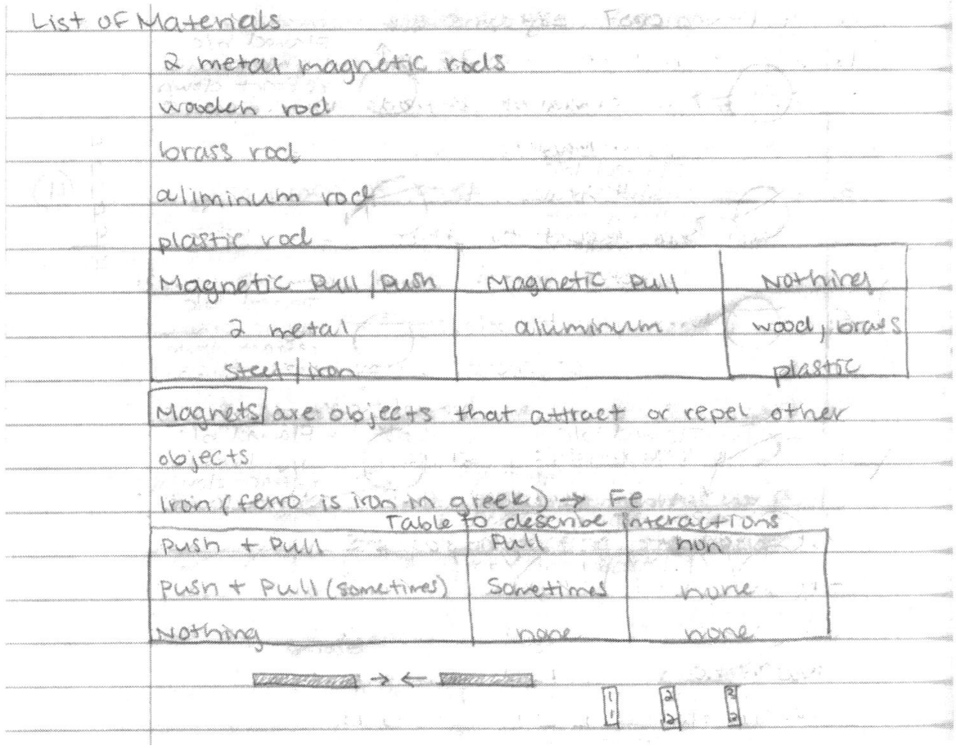

interactions, which they label 1. push, 2. pull, and 3. nothing. Objects that both push and pull each other they label as magnets. Objects that are pulled towards magnets but don't interact with each other or other things are called ferromagnets. Objects that don't interact at all are called non-magnets.

This is an excellent example where we get students to think about the *relevant* features during the recognition of a pattern. The first impulse of most students is to begin to place the cylinders into three groups:

1. metals,
2. plastics, and
3. woods.

However, when reminded that the task is sorting based on their interactions, they have to experiment, recognize that being a metal isn't relevant in and of itself to that sorting, and ultimately place the aluminum cylinder in the same pile as the wood cylinder. This is surprisingly uncomfortable for students. The iron ferromagnetic cylinders also look absolutely identical to the magnets (this was on purpose!), so they quickly learn that properties go beyond visual appearance.

The final question in Activity 4.2 is important. We want the student to make the connection between creating a taxonomy of magnetic interactions with the types of taxonomies they might build in other science disciplines. For example, in Chapter 2 I discussed how students could classify fish based on whether or not they have bones. Getting students to think about the ways that the thinking patterns they are using are applied in different contexts and how their thinking is really very similar serves as a metacognitive process essential for learning. Furthermore, this achieves our goal of reinforcing the crosscutting concepts within the NGSS, so that students can begin to realize that these concepts and thinking are universal tools that they can use in the future across disciplines. They're not learning stuff. They're learning how to learn stuff. There is a big difference between those two ideas, where the latter involves knowing, doing, and thinking.

Qualitative Patterns: Heat and Motion

In the previous section, we looked at teaching students to recognize patterns in observations. In the next two sections, we're going to look at teaching students to recognize and describe qualitative and then quantitative patterns in data. We're going to use the common concept of energy, both because it is a relatively abstract and tricky topic, and it is a crosscutting concept that we discussed in Chapter 2. In particular, we start the learning progression by having students participate in an investigation where they rub their hands together at varying speeds. With our elementary school class, we build a qualitative explanation from the observations in this investigation. From there, middle school students would use more sophisticated pattern recognition to develop a quantitative relationship between speed and energy. These ideas can then be applied to the even more abstract concept of waves.

Activity 4.3 shows a series of activities that you can do in the 4th grade classroom that starts by connecting the concept of energy to a concrete, directly measurable phenomenon (warm hands), and finishes with students using evidence they have gathered to address the following NGSS performance expectation (NGSS Lead States, 2013):

> 4-PS3–1. Use evidence to construct an explanation relating the speed of an object to the energy of that object.

Activity 4.3 Using Evidence to Explain the Relationship Between Speed and Energy

Part 1: Investigating Energy and Motion

Science Practice:

Conducting investigations

You're interested in investigating how energy can be related to motion. You will do this by rubbing your hands together at various speeds. Start by having each member of the group rub their hands together slowly and then quickly.

What did you notice when you rubbed your hands together?
Pattern Recognition:

What are common features you noticed between each group member's observations?

From this observation, come up with a way of measuring the energy. Also, come up with a way of measuring the speed of your hands. Your measurements only need to be qualitative, meaning you just need to be able to tell if you have more or less energy and speed than another measurement.

Record several observations by rubbing your hands together at four different speeds (slow, medium, fast, and superfast.) Also, record the energy you measure at these speeds (a little energy, more energy, a lot more energy, and super energy.)

Part 2: Graphing Energy as a Result of Motion

Science Practice:

Analyzing and interpreting data

You will now organize your data in a graph. A graph is a visual representation of your observations that will allow you to more easily see patterns and relationships.

The figure below shows how you will set-up your graph, with the amount of energy as the dependent variable, and the speed of your hands as the independent variable.

Figure 4.5 A graph of energy versus speed

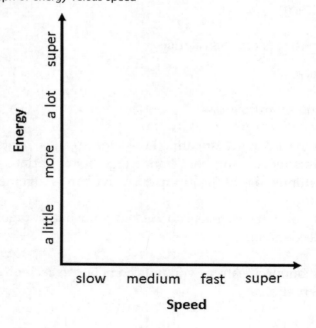

Fill in the graph using your observations for the energy.

Part 3: Explaining the Relationship

Science Practice:

Constructing explanations

Pattern Recognition:

Using your observations and your graph, what happens to the energy as you rub your hands faster?
   What evidence did you use to come up with this statement?
   What does this compare to?
   Can you think of other examples from everyday life that provide more evidence.

In Part 1, students observe that the palms of their hands get warmer as they rub their hands together. Using this observation, they conduct a short and simple investigation of the relationship between speed and energy. Notice that we are asking the student to determine how they intend to measure energy. Naturally, almost all of them will choose to measure how hot their hands get during rubbing as an indication of energy. Determining and articulating how a measurement will be made is a significant component of the science practice of planning and conducting investigations. I have bolded and underlined the science thinking pattern to make its use explicit. Notice how I used the framework of Thinking Task 4.1 to craft a question that is specific to this activity, but still serves as a reflective question on features within pattern recognition.

Once the students have recorded their observations, we move to Part 2 where the students now have data to visualize. If this is the first time you have worked with students in your classroom on graphs of data, then you will need to start off by modeling how it is done. In this case, Part 2 would be a modeled exercise. Otherwise, with more and more instruction, you should allow students more and more freedom to create their graphs. Part 2 results in a graphical representation of the relationship between energy and motion, from which the student can now extract a pattern.

In Part 3, students interpret their graphs to explain the relationship between the speed of an object and the energy of the object. They do this by articulating a statement about the relationship such as the following:

As the speed of an object increases its energy increases.

We are being explicit about what they are doing here: recognizing and identifying the pattern they see in the visualized data. They are also starting to think about relationships between variables *functionally*, which we'll discuss in greater depth in the next chapter.

Finally, we want to connect their observations of energy and its relation to motion to other examples from their day-to-day lives. For example, falling off a bike moving slowly versus moving fast. Catching a baseball pitch. Does a fastball hurt your hand more? Does it make a louder thud in the glove? Again, pulling examples from the student's experience provides that student with ownership of the observation. The student *discovers* the link between speed and energy. The student *creates their own* concrete understanding of energy: hot hands, scrapped knees, and louder smashing sounds. They aren't being told science content by an expert, they are discovering science content through their own experiences and observations. Furthermore, what we are doing here is building a prototype for energy within the students mind, so that it becomes easier in the future to recognize situations and/or phenomenon that are similar and make connections.

Quantitative Patterns: Representations of Data

Activity 4.3 was a qualitative activity for a 4th grade class. As students progress through the grade levels, the practices and thinking patterns stay the same, but their application becomes more sophisticated. In the previous example, we discussed students making qualitative measurements and graphing them qualitatively. The best they could do is tell whether something got bigger or smaller, but not by how much. In middle school, we start developing more sophisticated pattern recognition abilities. Therefore, we can begin to look at relationships more quantitatively.

Activity 4.4 uses simulated data to address the following NGSS performance expectation (NGSS Lead States, 2013):

MS-PS3–1.   Construct and interpret graphical displays of data to describe the relationships of kinetic energy to the mass of an object and to the speed of an object.

Activity 4.4   Analyzing and Interpreting Data to Determine what Affects the Kinetic Energy of an Object

Part 1: Graphical Displays of Data

Science Practice:

Analyzing and interpreting data

Skills:

Using a computer to graph data

(a) Speed and kinetic energy of a wagon

Speed (m/s)	Kinetic energy (J)
1	1
2	4
3	9
4	16

(b) Mass and kinetic energy of a wagon

Mass (kg)	Kinetic energy (J)
1	2
2	4
3	6
4	8

The tables above provide data for

(a) the kinetic energy of a wagon with a fixed mass going at different speeds, and
(b) the kinetic energy of the same wagon going a fixed speed but with different masses.

Create a scatter plot graphical display for each set of data, where the kinetic energy is the dependent variable and the speed and mass are the independent variables.

Part 2: Recognizing Patterns in Data

Science Practice:

Analyzing and interpreting data

If the mass of the wagon doubles, by how much does the kinetic energy go up?
If the mass of the wagon triples, but how much does the kinetic energy go up?
If the speed doubles, by how much does the kinetic energy go up?
If the speed triples, but how much does the kinetic energy go up?
Predict the kinetic energy of the wagon if it has a mass of 5kg.
Predict the kinetic energy of the wagon.

In Part 1 of this simple activity, students are given raw simulated data for the kinetic energy of a wagon having different masses and speeds. They then created a graphical display of the kinetic energy as a function of the mass, and then another display of the kinetic energy as a function of the speed. They do this using a computer and spreadsheet software. The use of software like this is a skill (as opposed to an ability); therefore, before completing this activity, you will want to have modeled how to use the spreadsheet software and how to create a basic two-dimensional scatter plot. This activity is an excellent opportunity for the student to begin independently practicing this skill.

Figure 4.6 shows example graphs created by a student for both relationships. Good graphical displays of data always include labels for the axes including units. In this particular example, a scatter plot (as opposed to a bar chart) is the most appropriate, as well, since we are trying to recognize

Figure 4.6 An example of student work graphing simulated data

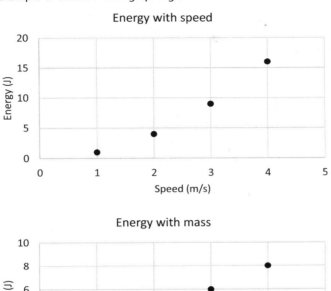

patterns. Good modeling will always include these characteristics so that students can develop skill at graphing data. The skill is required in order for students to progress to obtaining the ability to interpret the graph.

In Part 2 of the activity, we begin the process of teaching students how to recognize patterns in data beyond simple increase/decrease relationships. Specifically, when students interpret the mass/energy relationship, they see a simple proportional relationship. In class, you can also highlight the shape of the curve such a relationship exhibits in a graphical display (a straight line) so that they will easily be able to recognize it in the future.

The relationship between the speed and kinetic energy is less obvious. The activity leads students to recognizing the pattern through a series of questions:

◆ If the speed doubles, by how much does the kinetic energy go up?
◆ If the speed triples, but how much does the kinetic energy go up?

Working in teams, your students will discover from the graphical display and the raw data that the kinetic energy increases by four and then by nine and then again by 16. Some students will recognize this as a square relationship, where the kinetic energy is equal to the square of the speed, or more simply the speed times the speed. Other students and/or groups will require more coaching to arrive at this pattern. The square relationship arises frequently in physical science, so as the student develops they will encounter this pattern more and more, until it becomes more easily recognized.

When you first start working with your students on quantitatively recognizing patterns in data, then I recommend starting with simulated data as opposed to real data obtained by the student. With simulated data like that seen in Activity 4.4, you can control what the data looks like, so you can make the relationship easier for the student to recognize with less intervention. Then, you can tie that relationship to a specific curve shape (a prototype) on a graph that students can more easily recognize in the future. In future lessons, students will have more practice with recognizing similar patterns and will be able to work with more complex and less clear data sets.

The curves underlying graphical displays like those shown in Figure 4.6 are a type of mathematical representation students can use to make predictions. In Part 2, when the student is extrapolating the given data to determine the kinetic energy for mass and speed outside of the supplied data, they are using mathematical thinking. As mentioned above, the act of graphing the data is a skill. However, being able to look at the graph and determine a pattern and then use that pattern to make a prediction is an ability that requires significant intervention to develop.

Let's quickly look at how we would weave assessment of thinking into or normal assessment of the activity, keeping in mind that the *knowing-doing-thinking* framework requires assessment across the three dimensions simultaneously. Table 4.2 shows the generic NGSS evidence statements for the science practice of mathematical thinking. The NGSS expects students to be able to identify the characteristics of a simple mathematical representation and apply the representation to a physical system to identify how it corresponds to physical observations. They also must use the mathematical representation to identify patterns and make predictions based on changing parameters. I have highlighted the thinking pattern in Table 4.2 to make it clear where assessment of thinking fits into the overall assessment scheme. The rubric you build to assess the activity should have pattern recognition built in as a specific criterion.

TABLE 4.2 EVIDENCE STATEMENTS FOR USING MATHEMATICAL THINKING

The student . . .	
1	identifies the characteristics of a simple mathematical representation
2	applies the mathematical representation to a physical system to identify how the model characteristics correspond to physical observations
3	uses the mathematical representation to *identify patterns*
4	uses the mathematical representation to make predictions based on changing parameters

Source: Adapted from NGSS Lead States, 2013

Now let's think about how the activity lines up with the evidence statements. In the activity we have students identify how energy is affected by changes in physical characteristics of the wagon. Specifically, they can identify that the energy increases as mass and speed increase. For mass, they can quickly identify a linear increase using the mathematical representation of the graph. For the speed, they can identify a non-linear relationship, where the energy makes bigger increases for each interval that the speed increases. By looking at the raw data, they should also be able to identify the pattern with more precision, by recognizing that the kinetic energy is equal to the speed times the speed.

Notice that this final recognition can be facilitated by your choice of data. I intentionally designed the data to make this relationship more obvious. In future lessons, we would either use messier real data, or I would begin to simulate data where the relationship was less obvious. In these future lessons, the student now has to know to look for a pattern and have enough experience to know what types of relationships to look for. They will be successful if we slowly, methodically, and explicitly build the necessary prototypes in their mind on which to match future observations.

We'll talk about creating predictive models in the next chapter, but I want to highlight that the thinking done when recognizing patterns is the first step in the hypothesis/model generation process. Once the student determines the pattern in the data, they now have a model on which to base a prediction. For the example of changes in mass, the student can now predict that increasing the mass by one more kilogram will result in an energy that goes up by 2 Joules. Similarly, they will be able to predict that a speed of 5 meters per second will result in an energy of 5 times 5 Joules (25J). This recognition can lead to a more formal mathematical model. In fact, if done well, your students *can discover* that the energy is proportional to the mass times the square of the speed, before ever seeing that relationship in a book.

I want to show you one more follow-up activity that connects the doing and thinking within a slightly different context. This might be an activity or assessment you could use at a later time in your class. Imagine that your students have been introduced to graphing, data interpretation, and quantitative pattern recognition. Now, let's see an activity where they use all of this within a different context. Activity 4.5 shows a simple set of multiple choice questions designed by the Stanford NGSS Assessment Project for the following NGSS performance expectation (Dozier, 2017; NGSS Lead States, 2013):

> MS-PS4–1. Use mathematical representations to describe a simple model for waves that includes how the amplitude of a wave is related to the energy in a wave.

Activity 4.5 Mathematical Thinking with Energy and Waves

Adapted from Dozier, 2017

The graph below shows the relationship between the amount of energy transferred by an ocean wave and its amplitude.

Figure 4.7 The relationship between the amounts of energy transferred by an ocean wave and its amplitude

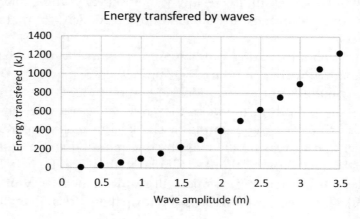

A company is deciding where to build a plant to generate electricity from ocean wave energy. Individual waves at any location vary in size, so the company measured waves at two locations and calculated the average wave amplitude, shown in the table below.

Location	Wave amplitude	Energy transferred
A	2 meters	500 kJ
B	4 meters	???

1. Use the graph and the table above to estimate the amount of energy transferred at location B.

   A. 300 kJ
   B. 400 kJ
   C. 800 kJ
   D. 1,600 kJ
   E. 3,200 kJ

2. Using the data above, describe the difference between the amplitude of an average wave in each location.
      Compared to location A, an average wave in location B . . .

   A. is taller from the bottom to the top of the wave
   B. has less energy
   C. has more distance between it and the next wave
   D. has less distance between it and the next wave

3. How does the energy transferred by a wave change when the energy is doubled?
      The energy transferred . . .

   A. decreases slightly
   B. increases slightly
   C. doubles
   D. more than doubles

Designed and validated by Ph.D. student Sara Dozier, this short and simple activity examines the student's ability to go through a similar process as that in Activity 4.4, only this time in the context of energy and waves.

Data for the relationship between the wave amplitude and the amount of energy transferred is provided in a graphical form. The first question asks the student to use the graph to estimate the energy for a wave amplitude that is not explicitly provided for in the data. To accomplish this, the student must identify the characteristics of the energy/amplitude relationship from the graph: the energy goes up more and more with each interval increase in amplitude. They then must identify the pattern explicitly (again, a square relationship) in order to make a prediction about what the energy would be for an amplitude of 4 meters. If the student has successfully built a "square relationship" prototype in their mind, then this identification becomes much easier.

In the first question, it is possible for the student to determine a correct answer with no content knowledge on waves. The axes could read "banana" and "orange" and the student could still recognize the pattern in the data. The second question assesses the combination of the student's content knowledge and ability to interpret the graph. In particular, to answer correctly, the student must identify the amplitude as the bottom-to-top distance and distinguish it from the frequency. Furthermore, they must recognize from the data that the wave amplitude is greater at location B.

The last question in the activity once again checks the student's ability to identify the pattern. Rather than simply extrapolate to 4 meters, they are given a more generic question concerning a doubling of the amplitude. Note that in order to answer all of the questions correctly, the student needs to synthesize content knowledge, practice abilities, and science thinking. Therefore, this is an excellent example of a three-dimensional activity, or it could be used an assessment of three-dimensional learning.

Summary

In summary, we looked at how pattern recognition develops at a young age, and the implications that development has for teaching and learning. I more specifically defined pattern recognition and discussed the various models psychologists and cognitive scientists have for what goes on in our mind with respect to pattern recognition. Ultimately, the three basic components of pattern recognition are templates, prototypes, and features. The synthesis of specific features into sets form prototypes that we can match with new stimuli. The Thinking Task was developed to help guide this synthesis process and serve as an easy way to incorporate explicit pattern recognition into your lessons.

Our goal is to improve pattern recognition abilities, and you learned to do this by explicitly naming them, getting students to think about what their minds are doing in the process, and looking at strategies for assessing students' thinking with respect to patterns. To that end, I provided several example activities. I started by discussing the importance of explicit work with switching between multiple representations of the same phenomenon, and then using shared features to create taxonomies. I then showed you examples of activities designed to help develop both qualitative and quantitative pattern recognition throughout grade levels. In all of these activities, we made pattern recognition explicit, we had the student reflect on their own thinking, and we made thinking count.

The following is a brief summary of the main points:

- The ability to order and distinguish items starts at around 4 and develops until around 8 years of age.
- Having students work on pattern recognition tasks improves abilities and learning in other areas.
- Science lessons are excellent opportunities to incorporate pattern recognition into student learning.
- For our purposes, the three basic components of pattern recognition are as follows:
    - ◇ templates
    - ◇ prototypes, and
    - ◇ features.

- The synthesis of specific features into sets form prototypes that we can match with new stimuli.
- The foundation of a thinking task for pattern recognition is the following three questions:
    - ◇ Where have you seen this before?
    - ◇ What does this compare to?
    - ◇ What features are relevant and what else has these features?

- Explicit work on switching between multiple representations of the same phenomena is necessary and important.
- Creating taxonomies requires the recognition of shared features.
- Create activities that develop pattern recognition qualitatively and quantitatively.

References

Chi, M., Feltovich, P., & Glaser, R. (1981). Categorization and representation of physics problems by experts and novices. *Cognitive Science, 5*, 121–152.

Dozier, S. (2017). *Energy and Ocean Waves.* Retrieved from Stanford NGSS Assessment Project: http://web.stanford.edu/group/ngss_assessment/cgi-bin/snapgse/

Eysenck, M., & Keane, M. (2003). *Cognitive Psychology: A Student's Handbook* 4th ed. New York: Taylor & Francis.

Inhelder, B., & Piaget, J. (1969). *Early growth of logic in the child.* New York, NY: W. W. Norton & Company, Inc.

Kidd, J., Curby, T., Boyer, C., Gadzichowski, K., Gallington, D., Machado, J., & Pasnak, R. (2012). Benefits of an intervention focused on oddity and seriation. *Early Education and Development, 23*(6), 900–918.

Larkin, J. (1985). Understanding, problem representations, and skill in physics. *Thinking and Learning Skills, 2*, 141–159.

Larkin, J., & Simon, H. (1987). Why a diagram is (sometimes) worth ten thousand words. *Cognitive Science, 11*, 65–99.

Mattson, M. (2014). Superior pattern processing is the essence of the evolved human brain. *Frontiers in Neuroscience, 8.*

McDermott, L. C. (1996). *Physics by Inquiry.* New York: John Wiley & Sons.

Moore, J. C., & Rubbo, L. J. (2012). Scientific reasoning abilities of nonscience majors in physics-based courses. *Physical Review Special Topics – Physics Education Research, 8*, 010106.

Moore, J., & Slisko, J. (2017). Dynamic Visualizations of Multi-body Physics Problems and Scientific Reasoning Ability: A Threshold to Understanding. In T. Greczylo, & E. Debowska (eds), *Key Competences in Physics Teaching and Learning.* New York, New York: Springer.

NGSS Lead States. (2013). *Next Generation Science Standards: For States, By States.* Washington, DC: The National Academies Press.

Piaget, J., & Szeminska, A. (1941). *La genèse du nombre chez l'enfant* [*The development of numbers in children*]. Neuchâtel, France: Delachaux and Niestlé.

Shugen, W. (2002). Framework of pattern recognition model based on the cognitive psychology. *Geo-spatial Information Science, 5*(2), 74–78.

Silva, J. (2011). On Creativity, Marijuana and "a Butterfly Effect in Thought". *Huffington Post.*

5

What's Important, What's Not, and Designing a Fair Test

"Fools ignore complexity. Pragmatists suffer it. Some can avoid it. Geniuses remove it."
—Alan Perlis (Perlis, 1982)

We live in a very complex world. From our very birth, we are bombarded with complex shapes and images, all engaging in fits of non-linear motion. We cognitively adapt to this stimuli-based complexity rather quickly in our day-to-day lives, but the problems and challenges we face are often composed of and influenced by a vast number of variables. A problem as simple as determining which route you should take in your drive to work can be surprisingly complex, possibly requiring many considerations such as time of day, time of year, construction schedules, fuel costs, personal stress levels, and how much sleep you got the night before. As we discussed in the last chapter, pattern recognition is arguably the foundation of human thought (Mattson, 2014). However, recognizing patterns becomes exceedingly difficult the more variables are added and the more complex their relationships become.

In this chapter, we're going to discuss how scientists attempt to reduce complexity so that they can begin to see the patterns we discussed previously and begin to make sense of the world. Specifically, we're going to look at two science thinking patterns: causative thinking and control of variables. Control of variables involves both the recognition of relevant variables, and being able to systematically isolate those variables in observations so that patterns can be seen. Causative thinking uses control of variables and resulting patterns to make determinations about the causal link between events.

First, I'm going to describe the research on both causative thinking and control of variables. We will use that research and the *explicit-reflective-count* framework from Chapter 3 to inform practical "Thinking Task" worksheets (a set of questions) that you can incorporate into any lesson where these thinking patterns are used. Finally, I'll show you several activities that involve causative thinking and control of variables and discuss how the thinking tasks can be easily built into the lessons. We'll start by looking at activities where students must recognize relevant variables and distinguish them from irrelevant variables in the context of a particular scientific question. Then, I'll show you several activities covering different content where students isolate variables in experiments to determine what patterns might arise and what might be the causes. We'll end the chapter by discussing how the combination of control of variables, pattern recognition, and causative thinking allows the student to induce hypotheses. Basically, we're going to learn the thinking behind how scientists come up with hypotheses and how that can be taught in the classroom.

Causation and Causative Thinking

Patterns have causes, which can be simple or complex and a function of multiple variables. Part of science thinking is investigating and explaining these causal relationships. Does doing this thing over here *cause* that result over there? Sometimes, we notice repeating patterns that seem influenced by some factor, but that factor might not be the cause. It's correlative but not causative. In the example we used in Chapter 1, you noticed that plastic bottles of soda keep exploding when you leave them in the trunk of your car. You could conclude that trunks cause soda bottles to explode. But was the trunk itself the cause? How would you be able to find out? Are there other variables in play? What is the real causative mechanisms and can it be tested?

The idea of causation is useful in the scientific and everyday world because we use such relationships to predict what will happen next. These causal links can guide our lives. For example, the fastest driving route to work may *not* be the best route because it also may be the most stressful. Personally, I've learned that I don't hate the driving itself, but I do hate driving with other cars around. The traffic *causes* me stress not the driving, so I will go out of my way and actually spend longer on the road to avoid being around too many other cars. Being able to make the causal link between traffic and stress versus driving and stress is an example of causative thinking applied to day-to-day life. In scientific research causation is similarly important because scientists can use such relationships to make predictions about experimental outcomes. Causative mechanisms can help us *explain* why relationships between variables exist.

Most studies of students' causative thinking ability have focused on what is called "inductive causal inference," where researchers focus on how a student goes about inferring patterns from evidence and compares their thinking to the thinking process of experts (Kuhn, 1989). The mental "rules" that we use to make causal inferences seem to emerge in childhood and remain established well into adulthood (Koslowski & Masnick, 2002). The only significant difference between how the child infers causal links compared to the adult is a greater ability to differentiate between causes and to consider a greater amount of information when making judgments. This could be the result of more experience leading to more mental prototypes for comparison. The basic rules, though, are pretty much the same.

What defines those rules in the psychological sense and what constitutes evidence of causation in the philosophical sense are still highly debated. However, we can extract some basics from looking at the research that we can then use to *practically* inform our teaching. There is enough consensus on causation and enough research on how to teach thinking causatively for our classroom purposes. We'll leave the remaining debates to the psychologists and philosophers.

To begin thinking about causation, we have to go all the way back to the philosopher David Hume, who identified the concept of "covariation" in experience (Hume, 2008). Covariation in this sense is the observation that one variable reliably changes as a response to a change in another variable. In fact, Hume's basic conclusion was that we can have no *ultimate* understanding of the physical world, only a psychological understanding based on experience and observation of covariations. I'm not smart enough to argue with David Hume, so I won't in this book. What is interesting, though, is that past research on the thinking of young children (who have obviously not read Hume!) shows that they have a natural tendency to use the covariation of events as an indication of causality (Schulz & Gopnik, 2004; Shultz & Mendelson, 1975).

However, more recently Cornell educational psychologist Barbara Koslowski has questioned the fundamental primacy of covariation evidence in science education. Science is not only about the discovery of causes, but also about the attempt to determine the causal mechanisms (Koslowski, et al., 1989). What is the actual physical process that is happening to link the cause with the effect? We live in a world full of correlations that are not necessarily causative, and according to Koslowski, it's through consideration of the underlying mechanisms that we can determine which correlations also happen to be causative.

Humorist author Tyler Vigen has produced an entire book of ridiculous correlations called *Spurious Correlations* (Vigen, 2015). As an example from his book, Figure 5.1 shows that there is an incredibly strong correlation ($r = 0.95$) between the per capita cheese consumption in the USA and the number of people who died by becoming tangled in their bedsheets (Vigen, 2018). (I would *love* to find correlations that strong in my own work!) Hume might argue that the only real meaning we could draw from these observations is that the two variables are covariant. Koslowski would point out that the relationship is spurious because there is no causal mechanism that ties them together. I think everyone will agree that 800 deaths by bedsheet per year is a lot!

A less ridiculous example would be the correlation between hamburger consumption in a society and the prevalence of illness. There is a correlation, but if hamburger consumption is *the cause* of increased illness, then there has to be a causal mechanism. In this particular case, there are several potential mechanisms, with the *e. coli* bacterium being one of them (Hu & Willett, 1998).

The Thinking Lab at Yale University has shown that most adults "seek out and prefer information about causal mechanisms rather than information about covariation," which was in contrast to earlier work that we might call "Hume-like" (Ahn, et al., 1995). Koslowski's recent research and the work of others has supported this idea, and they have shown that even young children hold complex causal theories about phenomena that include covariation, theoretical causal mechanisms, and possible alternative causes (Koslowski & Masnick, 2002; Schulz & Gopnik, 2004).

Figure 5.1 Graph showing the spurious correlation between per capita cheese consumption in the USA and the number of deaths per year by entanglement in bedsheets. Other funny spurious correlations can be found at the following website: www.tylervigen.com/spurious-correlations

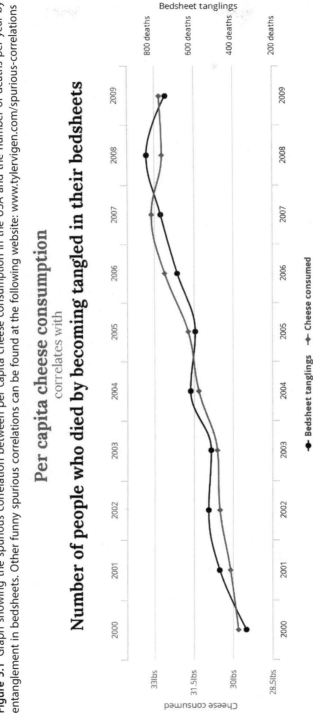

Per capita cheese consumption
correlates with

Number of people who died by becoming tangled in their bedsheets

Source: Adapted from Vigen, 2018

Fundamentally, what we can learn from this discussion is that there are two aspects to our thinking with respect to causation:

1. covariation, and
2. a linking mechanism.

I've provided some good examples of causal mechanisms; however, we still need to define causes and covariations themselves more explicitly.

In general, causes may be distinguished into three types (Riegelman, 1979; Epp, 2004):

1. *necessary*,
2. *sufficient*, and
3. *contributory*.

These three types of causes are described in Table 5.1. Necessary causes are required for a certain result. For example, the sun rising is a necessary cause of daytime. If you look up and notice that it is daytime, then it is necessary that at some point earlier the sun rose. Sufficient causes produce a certain result, but something else could have also produced the same result. Not eating for several hours is a sufficient cause of my hunger. However, my hunger could have also been caused by running for 30 minutes. Therefore, even though not eating causes hunger, being hungry doesn't necessarily mean I haven't eaten. A contributory cause contributes to some result, but is neither necessary nor sufficient. For example, being tired could contribute to me being angry. Just because I'm angry, though, doesn't mean I'm tired, so it's not a necessary cause. Also, being tired by itself doesn't necessarily lead to anger, so it's not a sufficient cause. More

TABLE 5.1 THE THREE TYPES OF CAUSES

Cause	Description
Necessary	Causes that are required for a certain result. If A is a necessary cause of B, then an observation of B requires that A happened.
Sufficient	Causes that produce a certain result, but something else could have also produced the same result. If A is a sufficient cause of B, then A happening requires B to follow; however, an observation of B doesn't require that A was the cause, since C also causes B.
Contributory	Causes that contribute to some result, but are neither necessary nor sufficient. If A is a contributory cause of B, then some other cause C must also be present.

than likely, anger will result from the combination of multiple contributing factors, such as being tired, hungry, and stressed.

Combining an understanding of the types of causes with a constant search for causal mechanisms results in a rich model for thinking about how things and experiences are related. From the research I have cited, we know that our students are already thinking about these aspects when they evaluate information. However, as I've pointed out again and again, our focus in our teaching needs to be on getting students to think about their thinking. With a good understanding of how students and adults think about causation, we can begin to create metacognitive activities that we can do with our students that are explicit, reflective, and assessable.

Control of Variables

Before we get into those activities, we need to first discuss control of variables. To understand how different variables might affect patterns, and therefore causation, the scientist must be able to control those variables within their minds as well as in practice as they design experiments to probe the how and why of a pattern and/or a covariation (Chinn & Hmelo-Silver, 2002). Does hunger lead to anger? When? What conditions are necessary? What other variables might be relevant to anger?

Most of scientific inquiry involves processes of many variables, even at some of the simplest levels. Most if not all of the variables need to be identified and the relationships between the variables need to be determined to begin to infer what is going on. In other words, scientists control variables in an effort to make complex stuff less complex.

Most control of variables strategies have two components, which are described in Table 5.2 and are as follows:

1. the *recognition* of relevant variables, and
2. the ability to *isolate* those variables in experiments.

TABLE 5.2 THE TWO COMPONENTS OF CONTROL OF VARIABLES THINKING

Cause	Description
Recognition	Recognizing and explicitly identifying the relevant variables in a complex system.
Isolation	Isolating relevant variables to determine one-to-one relationships between variables with as few confounding factors as possible.

Returning to our exploding bottles example, you notice that the plastic bottles of soda in your trunk only seem to expand and explode in your car trunk during hot summer months. You might rightly conclude that the temperature is a relevant variable. Moving forward, you could devise an experiment to explore the relationship. Isolation of variables means that you will try to limit or eliminate other possible influences while only changing the temperature. Maybe you ensure that the types of soda are kept consistent, or that the bottles all have the same shape and size, since these may also be relevant variables.

Sometimes, it's easy to recognize the relevant variables. However, this is not always the case in science. For example, most of the causes of health and disease or contributory, with some contributory causes being well hidden. *Epidemiological* studies attempt to determine possible causes and how much or how little those causes might contribute. In some such studies, just determining what the relevant variables are is the entire point of the research. Even after recognizing some relevant variables, complex systems like disease are often difficult to isolate, resulting is what we call a *confounded* experiment. Good total control of variables thinking can be used to distinguish significantly confounded experiments from highly controlled experiments, providing the scientist insight into how much to trust the result (a topic we'll look at in more detail in Chapter 7). Basically, the second component of control of variables, isolation, is the fundamental thinking underlying the design of un-confounded experiments from which valid, causal relationships can be determined (Chen & Klahr, 1999).

Within science education, control of variables has been deemed central to science instruction at the earliest of ages (Klahr & Nigam, 2004; Dean & Kuhn, 2007). However, there has been some interesting debate over how best to teach control of variables strategies.

David Klahr and Milena Nigam reported that direct instruction of control of variables strategies was more effective than an inquiry-based approach when working with 3rd and 4th grade students (Klahr & Nigam, 2004). In essence, the work of Klahr and Nigam suggests control of variables is a skill as opposed to a cognitive ability. A skill can be learned and then repeated without significant further development, with skills generally being best taught through direct instruction. An ability requires significant metacognition in-action to perform and is best developed over time via more constructivist methods.

David Dean and Deanna Kuhn, however, showed that when looking at the development of control of variables thinking over a longer period of time "direct instruction appears to be neither a necessary nor sufficient condition for robust acquisition or for maintenance" (Dean & Kuhn, 2007). Dean and Kuhn replicated the results of Klahr and Nigam, but they also looked at growth and development over several months and across multiple contexts. What they found is that direct instruction with elementary school children does not necessarily result in *transfer* of this ability from one context to another, nor does it result in *retention*. A combination of direct instruction and continual practice in authentic settings and across multiple contexts was necessary for transfer and retention.

My own research has shown results complimentary to Dean and Kuhn, only with college-aged pre-service elementary and middle school teachers (Moore & Rubbo, 2012; Moore, 2012). This suggests that there is significant difficulty with control of variables thinking throughout the grade levels, and that a combination of direct instruction and inquiry-based reflective practice can improve thinking across grade levels. Furthermore, all of this work combined highlights that control of variables thinking is an ability that must be nurtured, as opposed to a basic skill to learn. This research is part of the foundation for the *explicit-reflective-count* framework for teaching science thinking that we discussed in Chapter 3. Direct and explicit instruction combined with consistent reflective practice and assessment can result in the learning of science thinking.

Thinking Tasks: Causative Thinking and Control of Variables

Like we did in the previous chapter, we can use the educational and philosophical research we just discussed on causation and control of variables to inform an approach to getting students to think about what it is they are doing when completing tasks requiring these thinking patterns. We learned in Chapter 3 that student metacognition is *the* key to improvements in deployment of science thinking. We must get them to actively think about what they are thinking when engaged in science practice. To do this with respect to causation and control of variables, we can utilize the foundational pieces of each to inform questions that we can ask the student to ponder.

We will take a similar approach to that taken in the previous chapter, where we focus on a set of questions we can incorporate into activities. Thinking Task 5.1 shows such a short series of questions that we can insert into any lesson that includes causative thinking. This can be done as either a separate worksheet, the questions could be inserted into an existing worksheet, or you could simply ask these questions during the completion of the activity. As you will see in the example activities later in this chapter, you can also edit these questions to better fit your specific content. Either way, the question set serves as a metacognitive activity that forces reflection on causative thinking.

Thinking Task 5.1 Causative Thinking

What mechanism might connect these two ideas?

Could these ideas be connected via some other hidden idea?

Is the relationship between the ideas necessary, sufficient, or contributory?

The first two questions are informed by the breakdown of causative thinking into covariations and causal mechanisms, as we just discussed. The third question has the student think about the various types of causes that we have identified. The following lists each aspect together with the reflective question that was motivated by our previous discussion:

Causal mechanisms – what mechanism might connect these two ideas?

Causal mechanisms – could these ideas be connected via some other hidden idea?

Cause types – is the relationship between the ideas necessary, sufficient, or contributory?

Thinking Task 5.2 shows such a short series of questions that we can insert into any lesson that includes control of variables. The questions are informed by our breakdown of control of variables thinking into variable recognition and isolation. The following lists each aspect together with the reflective question:

Recognition – why is this variable relevant?

Isolation – can I measure this variable?

Isolation – can I control this set of variables?

Thinking Task 5.2   Control of Variables

Why is this variable relevant?
Can I measure this variable?
Can I control this set of variables?

The three basic principles we learned in the previous chapter for teaching science thinking were to be explicit, be reflective, and make thinking count. In the implementation of the thinking tasks, it is important to be explicit with what you are doing. You can do this through text like you see at the top of Thinking Tasks 5.1 and 5.2, or orally by consistently highlighting to students that what they are doing now is causative thinking and/or control of variables. By asking the questions in Thinking Tasks 5.1 and 5.2, we are forcing the student to be reflective about what was going on in their minds. You can do this formally through a worksheet with written responses, or informally through a class discussion. Finally, we will discuss how to make it count by looking at assessment for some of the example activities in the rest of this chapter.

Recognizing Relevant Variables: The Simple Pendulum

Before a student can make a judgement about causative relationships, they first have to get a handle on the relevant variables. Therefore, I'm going to start our discussion on weaving thinking into activities by looking at control of variables thinking. The first step in control of variables is recognition.

Activity 5.1 shows aspects of an activity that my group actually uses as an assessment of science practice and thinking abilities in our physical science courses for pre-service teachers (Moore, 2018). In this activity, students are given a small set of materials and are asked to design and conduct an experiment or series of experiments to determine what physical properties of a pendulum affect its period of motion.

Activity 5.1: Pendulum Challenge

Science Practice:

Planning and conducting investigations

A pendulum is a weight suspended from a pivot so that it can swing freely. Figure 5.2 shows a schematic diagram of a pendulum composed of a piece of string and an attached mass called a "bob". The string is attached to a fixed point on one end, and the bob on the other. When the pendulum points directly down (position A, Figure 5.2), the pendulum is said to be in equilibrium. When the bob is displaced to position B (Figure 5.2) with a taut string and released, the bob will swing forwards and backwards as shown in Figure 5.2.

The time it takes to make a complete swinging motion (going from point B to point C and then back to point B) is called the period. You are interested in what physical properties of the pendulum system affect the period.

The following materials will be provided to you:

◆ a one meter length of string
◆ five pennies
◆ sticky tape
◆ timing device

Part I: Recognizing and Isolating Relevant Variables

Control of Variables:

What is the dependent variable you would use for this experiment?

What physical properties of the pendulum system do you think are relevant?

Figure 5.2 Diagram of pendulum motion

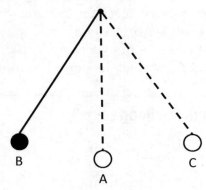

What independent variables would you assign to each property?

Why do you think each variable is relevant?

Can you measure each variable? If so, how?

Can you isolate the other variables while changing one variable? If so, how?

Part II: Design and Conduct an Experiment

Using the available equipment, design and conduct an experiment that provides data you can use to determine what affects the period and their relationships.

Part III: Cause and Effect

Causative Thinking:

Does it appear to you that any of the changes in properties cause a change in the period?

Did any properties not cause a change in the period?

What mechanism might connect properties that caused a change with the period?

Could the property and the period be connected via some other hidden idea?

Is the relationship between the property and period necessary, sufficient, or contributory?

In Part I of the activity, I have provided a series of questions that prompt the student to think about the physical properties that might have a reasonable effect on the period, how they would turn these physical properties into variables, and whether or not they can measure and isolate each variable. This series of questions is just a context-focused re-write of the questions in Thinking Task 5.2, where we're getting the student to explicitly focus on the variables and how they might isolate them. (As a side note, when we run this activity as a summative assessment, we don't actually make this line of questioning explicit. As a learning experience or formative assessment, though, the explicitness is suggested.)

How might we assess the thinking going on during this activity? As we discussed in Chapter 3, for NGSS-based assessment we can look at the specific evidence statements provided for the various science practices. Typically, we'll find the thinking buried in these evidence statements. As an example, Table 5.3 shows the generic evidence statements for conducting an investigation and evaluating design adapted from the NGSS (NGSS Lead States, 2013). The evidence statement where students demonstrate a recognition of variables is bolded, with assessment of isolation of variables highlighted by bold and underlined text. To think about how you might write specific criteria into a rubric based on these evidence statements, I encourage you to review Example 3.1, where I present a sample in the context of magnetism.

Another option for assessment that I want to point you to is the work done by the Rutgers University Physics Education Research Group. This group has developed a framework for teaching practice-based science that they call the Investigating Science Learning Environment (ISLE). They have several assessment tools and rubrics that have been developed over the years that perfectly align with our goals of assessing science thinking. Table 5.4 shows an example criterion for assessing variable recognition from

TABLE 5.3 EVIDENCE STATEMENTS FOR CONDUCTING AN INVESTIGATION AND EVALUATING DESIGN. WHERE STUDENTS RECOGNIZE VARIABLES IS BOLDED, AND WHERE STUDENTS ISOLATE VARIABLES IS BOLDED AND UNDERLINED

The student . . .	
1	**identifies the phenomenon to be investigated**
2	identifies evidence to address the purpose of the investigation
3	**plans the investigation**
4	collects the data
5	evaluates the design

Source: Adapted from NGSS Lead States, 2013

TABLE 5.4 EXAMPLE CRITERION FROM RUBRIC ON DESIGNING AND CONDUCTING OBSERVATION EXPERIMENTS

Ability	Missing	Inadequate	Needs improvement	Adequate
Is able to decide what physical quantities are to be measured and identify independent and dependent variables	The physical quantities are irrelevant.	Only some of the physical quantities are relevant.	The physical quantities are relevant. However, independent and dependent variables are not identified.	The physical quantities are relevant and independent and dependent variables are identified.

Source: From Etkina, et al., 2006

their larger rubric on observation experiments (Etkina, et al., 2006). Note that the larger rubric is designed to assess the science practice of designing and conducting experiments, and that some of the individual criteria within that rubric centers on the thinking patterns we have been discussing in this book. This is a concrete example of what we were discussing in Chapter 2: successful execution of science practice *requires* good science thinking.

Figure 5.3 shows an example of student work from their notebook when completing this activity. We can see that the student has identified the length of the string and the weight held at the end of the string as physical properties of the pendulum system that might affect the period. They have chosen to vary the length by folding the string to get measurements of 1, ¾, ½, and ¼ string lengths. They have chosen to vary the mass by changing the number of pennies, where the unit of measurement is "number of pennies." This particular student is demonstrating good recognition of relevant variables, and we can see some hints at how they intend to isolate those variables, as we'll discuss in the next section. If we were assessing this student based on the criterion from Table 5.4, the only thing missing would be an explicit identification of the dependent (period) and independent (length and mass) variables, resulting is a score of "Needs Improvement."

Figure 5.4 shows another example of student work for the same activity. From this example, we can see that the student has decided to measure the period for changes in the date on the penny. It is possible that the date on the penny could have some effect on the period. Maybe the mass of a penny varies as it gets older and collects dirt. However, when running this activity as a learning experience (as opposed to a summative assessment) I like to guide students to think about fundamentals and general system properties. For example, if the student thinks that the penny age might matter, I would probe their thinking on why they think the age matters. In some cases, the student is really struggling to identify any variable, so they went with the first "number" they see: the date. In other

Figure 5.3 Sample student work showing good recognition of relevant variables

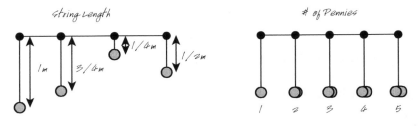

Figure 5.4 Sample student work showing recognition of an irrelevant variable

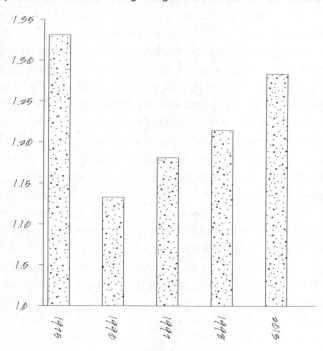

cases, they are thinking about the mass. If they are thinking about the mass fundamentally, then we guide them towards investigating the mass dependency directly.

Surprisingly, we have found that approximately 10% of students identify the date as the sole relevant variable during this activity, even after several weeks of explicit instruction and reflective practice. Only about 15% of student are able to identify at least two relevant variables for this experiment. This suggests that control of variables thinking and recognition of variables specifically is a fairly difficult thinking task. This is shown again and again in the research literature. A thinking process we as science instructors often take for granted requires significant intervention over time to develop (Dean & Kuhn, 2007).

Isolating Relevant Variables: The Simple Pendulum

After recognizing the relevant variables, students then have to think about how they will measure and isolate the variables. As shown in Table 5.3, isolation of variables thinking appears within the context of planning the investigation. We can see evidence of isolation thinking during the execution of the practice of planning.

Again, Figure 5.3 shows a student recognizing the relevant variables of mass and length. We get a glimpse of how the student plans to isolate the variables in the diagram that they draw. In the diagram they label as "string length," the number of pennies remains constant, in this case only one penny. In the diagram they label as "# of pennies," we can see that they have thought about keeping the length constant as they vary the number of pennies. If the student thinks that the mass is a relevant and potentially impactful variable with respect to the period, then they rightfully recognize that they must ensure that the mass does not change as they investigate the covariation between the length and period. Similarly, they maintain a constant length as they investigate the covariation between the mass and period.

Figure 5.5 shows the raw data as recorded by the same student. Even without written explanation from the student, we can see that they are properly isolating the variables of mass and length. For each length they measure the period for variations in the number of pennies. This provides the student with un-confounded data for the two independent variables (mass and length) covariate with the dependent variables (period). Figure 5.6 shows a graphical representation of similar raw data acquired by a different student in the same class. In this figure, we can see that the student also demonstrates an ability to estimate uncertainty as evidenced by the use of the error bars, which is something we'll discuss in more detail in Chapter 7.

Figure 5.5 Samples of student work properly isolating relevant variables

3/4 meter	Test 1	Test 2	Test 3
1 penny	1.465	1.465	1.495
2 pennies	1.515	1.65	1.615
3 pennies	1.65	1.645	1.575
4 pennies	1.555	1.595	1.65
5 pennies	1.555	1.575	1.475

Figure 5.6 Sample student work showing a graphical representation of data for the pendulum challenge

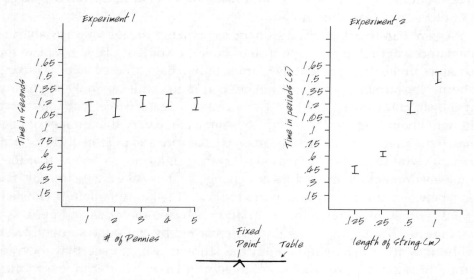

From the raw data and the graphical representations, these two students are able to form a judgement about the variables that they began the investigation believing to be relevant. Both students recognize that the mass of the pendulum "bob" does not seem to have any effect on the period, and that the length definitely does. In the first student's notebook, the following written summary is presented:

> *The amount of pennies added to the bob had little to no effect on the period of oscillation. The length of the string had a sizable effect on the period of oscillation.*

It turns out that the mass was not a relevant variable with respect to changes in the period of the pendulum. I want to be clear here: it is perfectly reasonable to have assumed its relevance before the experiment. In fact, what we are doing here is an *observation experiment*, where we're trying to determine exactly what is and isn't relevant or covariant.

Hypothesis Generation Through Observation

In Chapter 1, we talked about science as being composed of both inductive and deductive components. Scientists make simple observations, and from these observations they are able to determine relevant variables. In the case of our pendulum challenge, the students observed that the length was relevant and the mass was not. This was a type of *observation experiment*, or what science education researcher Eugenia Etkina calls a *hypothesis-generating experiment* (Etkina, et al., 2010).

Let's break this experiment down a little further. First, the students completing the pendulum challenge had to identify *potentially* relevant variables. The mass of the pendulum and the length of the pendulum are physical properties of the system that are general and changeable, so they make excellent potentially relevant variables. Another variable that may be of interest is the initial angle of release.

But what about the penny date? Why was this not relevant *a priori*? There are two reasons having to do with controllability and generalizability. First, the student has no real control of the date on the pennies. All five pennies are provided to the student and are selected randomly. Second, by investigating the date's covariation with the period, we are not necessarily answering the research question. The research question asks about a general pendulum and the properties of such. The date on pennies is a very specific, non-generalizable variable that would provide us no basic understanding of the system that we could use to make predictions about, say, a pendulum bob made of clay.

Figures 5.5 and 5.6 show two students determining relevant variables via an observation experiment, and then recognizing basic patterns in the observed data. For example, by representing the data like that shown in Figure 5.6, it becomes clear that a change in mass results in little to no change in period, whereas a change in length has a very profound change in the period. From this data alone it might be difficult to determine the exact mathematical relationship between the period and length, but it is the start for discovering such a relationship.

This is fundamentally the process scientists use to come up with a hypothesis. When conducting an observation experiment, a student focuses on investigating a physical phenomenon without having expectations of its outcomes. Again, scientists often have no clue what may or may not be relevant before beginning an investigation. Go back to Chapter 1 and look at Figure 1.3, which shows the more representative model of the scientific method. Notice that step one was asking a question. In this case, we were interested in what physical properties affect the period. We then use an investigation with control of variables and pattern recognition to determine what may and may not be relevant.

Armed with this information, we can now begin coming up with a hypothesis.

Figure 5.7 shows one of our students presenting a formal mathematical model for a pendulum and comparing the model to their observed results. The equation they present comes from some previously learned knowledge about pendulums, or they simply looked up information about pendulums. The student's actual data probably does not have enough resolution to come up with the relationship without prior knowledge. However, imagine the first scientist trying to "discover" the equation for a pendulum empiri- cally (as opposed to theoretically). They would have gone through the same process our student just completed, found the same relationships, maybe made very careful measurements, and then "fit" the length/period data to various mathematical models to find that the period is proportional to the square-root of the length.

Scientists (and our students!) are able to use inductive reasoning processes to ultimately develop a model or hypothesis for the physical system. First, they recognize potentially relevant variables, perform obser- vation experiments to determine relevance and covariations, examine the pattern in any observed covariation, and from the pattern develop a possible model. We'll discuss testing models and/or hypotheses in the next chapter.

Part of model/hypothesis building is thinking about causative relation- ships. Let's look at Part III of the activity, where we are looking for students

Figure 5.7 Student work showing a mathematical model of pendulum behavior compared with experimental data

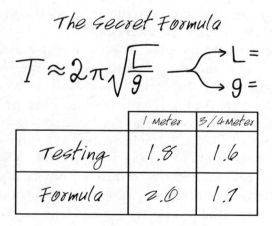

The Secret Formula

$$T \approx 2\pi\sqrt{\frac{L}{g}}$$

L =
g =

	1 Meter	3/4 Meter
Testing	1.8	1.6
Formula	2.0	1.7

to reflect on the cause/effect relationship between the length and the period. Mass did not cause a change in period. Length did cause a change in period. From the student-generated data alone, it's difficult to determine whether the length is a necessary cause or a contributory cause. Therefore, we have students think about what other variables could contribute, where you will hear things like air resistance, bob shape, string weight, etc. All of these could contribute to the period. Looking at the relationship our student highlights in Figure 5.7, the acceleration due to gravity is a contributory variable that we can change by, say, going to the moon. The key idea here is to get students to think about their thinking, their data, what it can and can't tell them, and what may or may not cause certain effects.

An Example from Light Reflection

Let's look at the two performance expectations for developing and using models within the context of light and its reflection, and how we can use the science thinking we have discussed up until now in concert with the practices. One performance expectation comes directly from the NGSS, while the other is an extension of the NGSS. They are as follows:

Students who demonstrate understanding can:

◆ 4-PS4–2. *Develop a model* to describe that light reflecting from objects and entering the eye allows objects to be seen.
◆ *Develop and use a model* for reflection to predict how light will behave when reflected off of a mirror.

We actually have to get the student to understand the development of a model for reflection *on the way* towards developing and using that model to understand how objects are seen. I discuss the learning progression for teaching light reflection in more detail in Chapter 4 of my book *Creating Scientists* (Moore, 2017). In what follows, we'll focus on weaving science thinking into the learning progression.

An example activity sheet for this progression is shown in Activity 5.2. In Part I, students construct a simple device that produces a thin beam of light, approximating a light "ray." They then aim the light beam at a plane mirror and sketch the resulting reflection for several different orientations of the mirror.

Activity 5.2   Ray Model of Light and Reflection

Part I: Observing Reflection Off a Plane Mirror

Science Practice:

Asking questions and making observations

Your group is going to build and use a simple device that makes a beam of light. This beam of light will allow your group to investigate light reflection. Figure 5.8 shows the device. It is made up of a flashlight and a piece of cardboard with a narrow slit. Build this device with the materials you have been given. Make sure it produces a very thin beam of light. (Note to teacher: you may wish to construct the cardboard pieces beforehand.)

Aim the beam of light at the mirror and observe what happens. First, aim the beam directly at the mirror. Next, turn the mirror and observe what happens to the beam of light. Each member of your group should take a turn playing with the mirror and light beam.

Document your observations in your scientific notebook using both pictures and words. As a group, write one or two sentences that explains what you have observed.

Control of Variables:

From your observation, if you wanted to learn more about how reflected light behaves, what variable(s) might be relevant?

Can you measure those variables?

After completing this part wait for further instruction from the teacher before moving to the next part. One representative from your group will present to the class during a class conference.

Figure 5.8 Schematic diagram of the lightbulb "ray" box

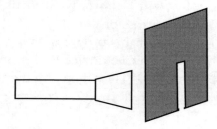

Part II: An Observation Experiment for Reflection Off Mirrors

Science Practice:

> Planning and conducting investigations/developing and using models

> Design and conduct an experiment that compares the incoming angle of a beam of light to the angle the reflected beam makes with a mirror. Control of Variables:

> What variable will you control (independent variable)?
> Which variable will you measure (dependent variable)?
> Document the experiment in your science notebook. Summarize your results using a table.

Figure 5.9 shows an example of student work for this part of the activity. Here, the process of observation is more "play-like" compared to the more formal variable recognition we had students do in the pendulum challenge. We simply ask them to play with the light box and mirror and make some general observations. This sets the stage for a discussion about what we might be able to measure to determine how the light ray incident on the mirror reflects.

Figure 5.9 Sample student work showing observations of light reflecting off of a plane mirror

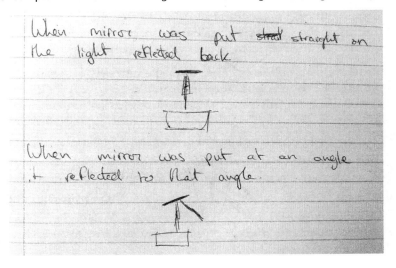

In Part II of the activity, the students design a more formal observation experiment to investigate how the angle that the incoming beam makes with respect to the mirror will affect the reflected beam. How you proceed depends on what skills you have already taught, like measurement of angles. If your students have never measured an angle before, then you'll have to teach that before they will even think about the angle as a potential variable.

First, students discuss in their groups how they will perform the experiment. Then, each group reports to the entire class on the process they want to use. You will guide this discussion, working with the class to develop a consensus procedure. An example would be aiming the beam at angles of 10°, 30°, 50°, and 70° with respect to the mirror, and then sketching the incoming and reflected beams for each. Then, students can measure the angle that the reflected beam makes with respect to the mirror. I like to have the students do these experiments on a large sheet of white paper. They can easily set up the equipment on the paper, and sketch the resulting beams, transferring the results into their scientific notebooks.

Figure 5.10 shows an image of student work in their scientific notebook. Notice that the student has organized their results in a table. After students have collected results, you will want to model for the students how to organize this data into tables, similar to the way the results are organized in Figure 5.10. I then like to have a representative from each group write their group's table of results on the board, so that we can then discuss and compare each group's results.

From this discussion, the students are able to recognize the very simple pattern: the incoming beam angle is roughly equal to the reflected beam angle. After all of the groups have written their results on the board, they should now be able to tell you the pattern, and therefore the model they can use for reflection. It is important that the students articulate the model themselves, so that they "own" it as opposed to having it dictated to them.

This entire process mirrors the process and thinking we used in the pendulum challenge. A question is posed: how does light reflect off of a mirror? Students play and observe. During their observations, they begin to recognize relevant variables. Once recognized, they can plan a more formal observation experiment with isolation of variables that investigates the relationship between incoming beam angle and outgoing beam angle. Finally, they can use the pattern recognized in the formal data to build a hypothesis: the incoming angle is equal to the outgoing angle. This hypothesis makes predictions that they can then test.

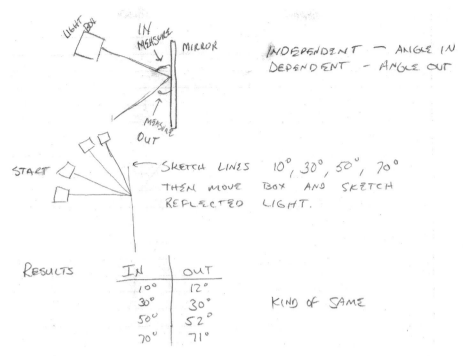

Figure 5.10 Sample student work showing the planning and results of a formal observation experiment. The angle the incoming beam makes with the mirror is found to be equal to the angle the outgoing beam makes with the mirror

Summary

In summary, I described the research on both causative thinking and control of variables and then presented activities helpful for teaching these thinking patterns. In particular, I used the research and the *explicit-reflective-count* framework from Chapter 3 to inform practical "Thinking Task" questions that you can incorporate into any lesson where these thinking patterns are used. I then showed you several activities that involve causative thinking and control of variables and discussed how the thinking tasks could be easily built into the lessons. In the activities, students recognize relevant variables and distinguish them from irrelevant variables in the context of a particular scientific question. Then, students isolate variables in experiments to determine what patterns might arise and what might be the causes. Finally, we discussed how the combination of control of variables, pattern recognition, and causative thinking allows the student to induce hypotheses.

The following is a brief summary of the main points:

◆ There are two aspects to our thinking with respect to causation:
  ◇ covariation, and
  ◇ a linking mechanism.

◆ Causes may be distinguished into three types:
  ◇ necessary,
  ◇ sufficient, and
  ◇ contributory.

◆ Most control of variables strategies have two components:
  ◇ the recognition of relevant variables, and
  ◇ the ability to isolate those variables in experiments.

◆ The foundation of a thinking task for causative thinking is the following three questions:
  ◇ What mechanism might connect these two ideas?
  ◇ Could these ideas be connected via some other hidden idea?
  ◇ Is the relationship between the ideas necessary, sufficient, or contributory?

◆ The foundation of a thinking task for control of variables is the following three questions:
  ◇ Why is this variable relevant?
  ◇ Can I measure this variable?
  ◇ Can I control this set of variables?

◆ Recognizing relevant variables is a fairly difficult cognitive task for students that must be developed over time through continual explicit instruction and reflective practice.

◆ Proper isolation of variables allows the student to determine which variables actually are and are not relevant, and how they relate to each other.

◆ Control of variables in an observation experiment can lead to hypothesis generation and the "discovery" of causal mechanisms.

References

Ahn, W. K., Kalish, C. W., Medin, D. L., & Gelman, S. A. (1995). The role of covariation versus mechanism information in causal attribution. *Cognition, 54*(3), 299–352.

Chen, Z., & Klahr, D. (1999). All other things being equal: Aquisition and transfer of the control of variables strategy. *Child Development, 70*(5), 1098–1120.

Chinn, C., & Hmelo-Silver, C. (2002). Authentic Inquiry: Introduction to the Special Section. *Science Education, 86,* 171–174.

Dean, D., & Kuhn, D. (2007). Direct instruction vs. discovery: The long view. *Science Education, 91,* 384–397.

Epp, S. S. (2004). *Discrete Mathematics with Applications* 3rd ed. New York: Brooks/Cole – Thomson Learning.

Etkina, E., Karelina, A., Ruibal-Villasenor, M., Rosengrant, D., Jordan, R., & Hmelo-Silver, C. (2010). Design and reflection help students develop scientific abilities: Learning in introductory physics laboratories. *Journal of Learning Sciences, 19,* 54–98.

Etkina, E., Van Heuvelen, A., White-Brahmia, S., Brookes, D., Gentile, M., Murthy, S., . . . Warren, A. (2006). Scientific abilities and their assessment. *Physical Review ST Physics Education Research, 2,* 020103.

Hu, F. B., & Willett, W. C. (1998). *The Relationship between Consumption of Animal Products (Beef, Pork, Poultry, Eggs, Fish and Dairy Products) and Risk of Chronic Diseases: A Critical Review.* Washington, DC: World Bank.

Hume, D. (2008). *An Enquiry concerning Human Understanding.* (P. Millican, ed.) Oxford: Oxford University Press.

Klahr, D., & Nigam, M. (2004). The equivalence of learning paths in early science instruction: Effects of direct instruction and discovery learning. *Psychological Science, 15,* 661–667.

Koslowski, B., & Masnick, A. (2002). The development of causal reasoning. In U. Goswami (ed.), *Blackwell Handbook of Childhood Cognitive Development* (pp. 257–281). Oxford: Blackwell Publishing.

Koslowski, B., Okagaki, L., Lorenz, C., & Umbach, D. (1989). When covariation is not enough: The role of causal mechanism, sampling method, and sample size in causal reasoning. *Child Development, 60,* 1316–1327.

Kuhn, D. (1989). Children and adults as intuitive scientists. *Psychological Review, 96,* 674–689.

Mattson, M. (2014). Superior pattern processing is the essence of the evolved human brain. *Frontiers in Neuroscience, 8.*

Moore, C. (2017). *Creating Scientists: Teaching and Assessing Science Practice for the NGSS.* New York, NY: Routledge.

Moore, J. (2018, July). Assessing practice and experiment design using a structured laboratory practical. *American Association of Physics Teachers Summer Meeting.* Washington, DC. Retrieved from www.creating scientists.com/research/

Moore, J. C. (2012). Transitional to Formal Operational: Using Authentic Research Experiences to Get Non-Science Students to Think More Like Scientists. *European Journal of Physics Education, 3*(4), 1–12.

Moore, J. C., & Rubbo, L. J. (2012). Scientific reasoning abilities of nonscience majors in physics-based courses. *Physical Review Special Topics – Physics Education Research, 8,* 010106.

NGSS Lead States. (2013). *Evidence Statements.* Retrieved from Next Generation Science Standards: www.nextgenscience.org

Perlis, A. (1982). Epigrams on Programming. *ACM SIGPLAN Notices, 17*(9), 7–13.

Riegelman, R. (1979). Contributory cause: Unnecessary and insufficient. *Postgraduate Medicine, 66*(2), 177–179.

Schulz, L., & Gopnik, A. (2004). Causal learning across domains. *Developmental Psychology, 40,* 162–176.

Shultz, T., & Mendelson, R. (1975). The use of covariation as a principle of causal analysis. *Child Development, 46,* 394–399.

Vigen, T. (2015). *Spurious Correlations.* New York: Hachette Books.

Vigen, T. (2018). *Spurious Correlations.* Retrieved from TylerVigen.com: www.tylervigen.com/spurious-correlations

6

Testing Our Crazy Ideas
with Experiments

"It does not make any difference how beautiful your theory is. It does not make any difference how smart you are – if it disagrees with experiment it is wrong. That is all there is to it."

—Nobel Prize winning physicist Richard Feynman (Feynman, 1965)

In the previous chapter, we found out how the combination of control of variables, causative thinking, and pattern recognition provide the thinking foundation for experiments that ultimately lead to new hypotheses and models. In this chapter, we're going to discuss the science thinking behind knowing whether those hypotheses and models are right. For the scientist, it isn't enough for their ideas to be "elegant" or "intriguing." Ideas in science must make predictions about the behavior of the real world, and scientists must be able to test those prediction. We're going to discuss the specific type of thinking a scientist does after hypothesis generation. Specifically, this chapter is about deductive thinking, where an idea is assumed and the consequences of that idea are deduced and matched with reality.

In particular, I will describe the types of experiments scientists do in more detail. We've already looked at observation experiments, but we haven't really defined them. We'll do that and expand our knowledge on experiments by discussing testing and application experiments. Then, we will look at the science thinking pattern called hypothetical-deductive reasoning, which is what goes on in the scientist mind as they think about what their hypotheses and models are trying to tell them about the world. We will use the research on the teaching and learning of hypothetical-deductive thinking and the *explicit-reflective-count* framework from Chapter 3 to inform a practical "Thinking Task" worksheet that you can incorporate into any lesson where this thinking pattern is used. Rather than a set of questions like we found in the previous chapter, the thinking task for hypothetical-deductive thinking is a general worksheet that guides student thinking across contexts. I'll show you how to use the worksheet in your class with several examples, and discuss the types of challenges students have with the worksheet and thinking in this way.

Hypothesis Testing and Experiment Types

Deanna Kuhn refers to scientific thinking as fundamentally the coordination of theory and evidence (Kuhn, 2004). For the purposes of this chapter, we're interested in how scientists coordinate their hypotheses and models with evidence obtained through experimentation, where success requires questioning existing explanations, seeking contradictory evidence, and eliminating alternative explanations.

In the next section, we'll discuss the science thinking pattern of hypothetical-deductive thinking, which is the name given to the reasoning process involved in this coordination. Before that, though, we need to talk about the various ways that evidence is acquired in experimental scientific investigations. Not all aspects of natural and physical science are experimental; however, the experiment is the ultimate arbiter of what does and does not happen in reality. Let's look at the types of experiments scientists do.

In the traditional view of the practice of science, all experiments appear to be epistemologically equal. That is to say, an experiment is an experiment. However, the analysis of the history of science and the work of scientists today shows that experiments can be grouped into different categories, each leading to some different type of knowledge. By studying scientists *in action* as opposed to what sociologist Bruno Latour calls "ready-made science," we can build a taxonomy of the types of experiments that they do (Latour, 1987).

Science education researcher Eugenia Etkina and colleagues have proposed that scientific experiments can be grouped into three big categories based on scientist *goals*, which are detailed in Table 6.1 (Etkina, et al., 2002). Similar to how we categorized materials based on their magnetic interactions to build a taxonomy in Chapter 4, we can group experiments based on the goals of the experimenter to build a taxonomy for experiments. Notice that we are not categorizing based on the disciplines (physics, chemistry, biology, etc.) or any specific methods. We are categorizing based on fundamental goals, which are shared across disciplines and are methodology independent.

The goals of scientific experimenters fall within one of the following basic categories:

1. they want to generate new ideas,
2. they want to test proposed ideas, and
3. they want to solve a practical problem.

We've discussed the generation of ideas in the previous chapter. How do we recognize relevant variables? What patterns emerge that could provide insight into underlying mechanisms? Often times, scientists have no clue what is going on and metaphorically (and sometimes literally) fiddle with

TABLE 6.1 THE THREE TYPES OF EXPERIMENTS WITH THE GOAL FOR EACH TYPE

Type	Goal	Description
Observation	Generate new ideas	The experimenter identifies and controls potentially relevant variables to determine what is and is not relevant, and how relevant variables relate. These experiments potentially lead to explanations, hypotheses, and/or models.
Testing	Test proposed ideas	The experimenter identifies a hypothesis or model to test, devises an experiment that could potentially falsify the hypothesis, and then makes a judgement based on the results. These experiments test explanations, hypotheses, and/or models, and can be used to distinguish between competing ideas.
Application	Solve practical problems	The experimenter uses well-tested ideas to solve a practical problem or determine an unknown value. These experiments use tested explanations, hypotheses, and/or models.

Source: Adapted from Etkina, et al., 2002

knobs and push buttons just to see what will happen. The observations that they make can lead them to potential explanations. Here, their goal is to learn what they don't know.

Once scientists have an idea or multiple ideas, they are then interested in testing those ideas. What do the ideas predict should happen in some new situation? Which ideas are successful? This is where scientists coordinate their hypotheses and models with evidence by questioning their ideas, seeking contradictory evidence, and eliminating alternative ideas. Here, their goal is to learn whether or not what they think they know is not wrong. ("Not wrong" is a clumsy way to say this in writing, but as we'll discuss later, it is a more accurate expression of the goal than "correct.")

Finally, science is used to solve problems. Once some of those science ideas are tested and re-tested until scientists have some confidence that they are not wrong, they can use these ideas to solve practical problems. For example, we know within certain constraints that Newton's Laws of Motion are not wrong, and we can use these ideas to build rockets that hoist massive satellites into orbit so that you can call your mother from anywhere on the surface of the Earth. Simpler examples include measuring the speed of light, or determining a specific reaction rate constant. Here, their goal is to use their "not wrong" ideas to solve a specific problem or answer a specific question.

Based on this compendium of goals we can classify experiments into the following three big groups (Etkina, et al., 2002):

1. observation experiments,
2. testing experiments, and
3. application experiments.

When conducting an observation experiment, the experimenter identifies and controls potentially relevant variables to determine what is and is not relevant, and how relevant variables relate. These experiments potentially lead to explanations, hypotheses, and/or models. For testing experiments, the experimenter identifies a hypothesis or model to test, devises an experiment that could potentially falsify the hypothesis, and then makes a judgement based on the results. These experiments test explanations, hypotheses, and/or models, and can be used to distinguish between competing ideas. In an application experiment, the experimenter uses well-tested ideas to solve a practical problem or determine an unknown value. These experiments use tested explanations, hypotheses, and/or models.

When discussing the distinctions between the different types of experiments in the classroom, getting students to think about their *expectations* for each type is a good idea. When conducting an observation experiment in the classroom, a student should focus on investigating a physical phenomenon without having expectations of its outcomes. When conducting a testing experiment, a student should have an expectation of its outcome based on concepts constructed from prior experiences. In fact, they will make a specific prediction for the outcome based on a hypothesis. In an application experiment, a student should use established concepts or relationships to address practical problems, with the expectation that the problem will be solved using the science.

Hypothetical-Deductive Thinking

Now, that we have a good understanding of the different types of experiments, we can look at the science thinking happening during the experimentation process. The science thinking involved in observation experiments was detailed in the previous chapter, and now you can integrate this with the more formal definition. For the rest of this chapter, we're going to look specifically at the thinking involved in testing experiments, or what we call hypothetical-deductive reasoning.

Once the scientist has observed and explored some pattern in nature and they discover some causal link between variables, they can begin to start explaining why the pattern happens with the ultimate goal of coming up with some model or hypothesis that they can use to predict future behavior. This type of mental activity is called hypothesis-generation, where the scientist uses their observations to form new hypotheses. The thinking pattern called hypothetical-deductive reasoning combines hypothesis-generation with control of variables to form a complete reasoning chain connecting the hypothesis to a specific test, result, and judgement. Ultimately, hypothetical-deductive reasoning is the thinking involved in hypothesis-testing.

Hypothetical-deductive thinking and its application can be divided into five stages as diagramed in Figure 6.1 and described as follows:

1. The student forms many hypotheses through the hypothesis-generation process, or conceptions based on previous experiences.
2. The student chooses a specific hypothesis to be tested.

Figure 6.1 The five stages of the hypothetical-deductive process

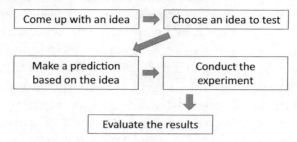

3. The student uses the hypothesis to make a previously un-observed predication.
4. The student uses the science practice of planning and conducting an experiment to check whether the prediction comes true.
5. From the results, the student evaluates whether the hypothesis is supported or not.

(Godfrey-Smith, 2003)

Students often have multiple ideas about how nature works based on their experiences throughout their lives. Some of these conceptions we call "alternative," since they aren't scientifically accurate. However, these ideas are not invalid, since research has shown that the student typically has formed them honestly based on their limited perceptions. Hypothetical-deductive thinking and the stages outlined above engages concept construction in a way where students can be free to have "crazy" ideas and allow the results of actual observations of the world to either support those ideas or not.

There are some limitations with respect to cognitive development you need to be aware of when working on hypothetical-deductive thinking in your classroom. In Jean Piaget's theory of cognitive development, hypothetical-deductive reasoning doesn't seem to appear until the formal operational stage, which doesn't begin until around the age of 11 (Inhelder & Piaget, 1969). In the past 50 years, continued research on the development of thinking has found that Piaget's model probably underestimates the capabilities of infants, preschoolers, and children in elementary school, and overestimates the adolescent's capabilities (Borke, 1975; Danner & Day, 1977). For example, some hypothetical-deductive reasoning appears to be possible at earlier ages, so long as the context remains directly observable. (This is a fancy way of me telling my elementary school teachers that they are not exempt from this science thinking pattern!)

Biologist and scientific reasoning specialist Anton Lawson has claimed that there are three general developmentally-based levels of hypothetical-deductive ability:

1. concrete,
2. hypothetical, and
3. theoretical.

(Lawson, et al., 2000)

These levels are based on the types of concepts involved in the hypothesis-testing. (This has the unfortunate result of a stage being called "hypothetical hypothetical-deductive thinking!") Concrete concepts are those ideas that have directly observable exemplars. Hypothetical concepts have observable exemplars, but are on scales far outside the everyday experiences of the scientist. Theoretical concepts have no directly observable exemplars.

For example, when creating a taxonomy of species of fish, we can directly observe the differences in the fishes on which the taxonomy is based. Answering the question "does this fish have bones?" requires only direct observation. Similarly, when playing with magnets, the student can directly experience the push and pull. The student conducting an investigation on a pendulum like we discussed in the previous chapter can directly observe and measure the mass, length, and time, all three relevant variables in the experiment. These are examples of concrete concepts that we can reasonably engage in hypothesis-testing with our younger students.

A student investigating the shrinking cells of an onion skin in saltwater can see the cells and observe their size using a microscope; however, they have to use significant imaginative faculties to conceive of the concept of un-observable charged water molecules leaving the cell due to some spooky attraction to charged sodium chloride molecules in the water. The student can directly observe the cells shrinking, but the causal agent is not directly observable. This would be an example of a hypothetical concept, where real stuff is transferring from the cell to the water, but the scale is outside of our direct perception. Similarly, strands of DNA, electrons and protons, and the size of Jupiter are all things that we could directly grasp were we a lot smaller or a lot bigger. Hypothetical concepts require well-developed proportional thinking, which is another one of our thinking patterns and an NGSS crosscutting concept. Hypothesis-testing on these types of concepts will be exceedingly difficult until the student has gained significant experience and has developed the cognitively ability to imagine the un-observable.

Finally, let's think about that spooky attraction between the water and salt molecules. Force as a concept has no observable exemplar no matter how small or large a size scale we could perceive. It isn't a "thing" like a cell at all. Similarly, energy has no physical substance. Both force and energy are concepts completely made up by scientists. They are useful concepts because they explain behavior we can observe, such as changing speeds of objects, objects getting hotter, and massive stuff requiring more effort to move. That's why scientists made them up. However, they cannot be directly observed, even though their effects can sometimes be indirectly observed. These are examples of theoretical concepts, and are the most difficult types on which to engage in hypothetical-deductive thinking.

If you look through the NGSS DCIs while thinking about the distinction between these types of concepts, you'll find that a lot of the science content we are expected to teach is either hypothetical or theoretical. Most of our work with elementary school students is confined to the concrete. However, as the student progresses through the grade levels, the way we approach content becomes more and more abstract, requiring greater and greater imagination and visualization ability to understand.

How Students Approach Hypothesis Testing

Multiple studies have shown that a student's ability to understand abstract science content depends on their developmental level and scientific reasoning ability (Lawson, et al., 2000; Coletta & Phillips, 2005; Moore, 2012; Moore & Rubbo, 2012). What this means is that Stages 3 and 4 from the 5 stages of the hypothetical-deductive process diagramed in Figure 6.1 are very challenging for students and require significant support structures, modeling, and coaching provided by the instructor. Students have difficulty coming up with useful testing experiments, for example, especially with content that is hypothetical, theoretical, or that they just don't quite understand.

Let's look at an example of where students often stumble in the hypothetical-deductive process during Stages 3 and 4. My research group examined how students responded when being individually tasked with relatively simple experimental questions (Moore, 2012). As an example from this study, we asked students to design an experiment that probed their ability to correlate a hypothesis on electric circuits with a reasonable testing experiment for that hypothesis. The question was as follows:

A single bulb circuit consists of a battery, two wires and a bulb arranged such that the bulb is lit. A student believes that it doesn't matter which way the "+" sign on the battery is oriented. Describe an experiment that the student can do to test their belief.

We posed this question to individual students before instruction and solicited open-ended answers. In previous courses, this specific question was part of the group learning experience. However, we quickly learned that it is easy for struggling students to appear to be making connections, when in fact they are merely parroting by rote the reasoning of other individuals in their group. This became apparent to us when we discovered students doing poorly on individual reasoning tasks post-instruction, when during participation in class they seemed to correctly approach the activities requiring these abilities.

Individual student responses were grouped, with the following five statements representing typical student responses to the question:

S1: The orientation of the battery does not matter, so rebuild the circuit in exactly the same way to show that the orientation does not matter.

S2: Conduct a controlled experiment, varying only the number of batteries to see if that makes a difference.

S3: Redo the experiment, but make sure it is controlled by holding all independent variables constant; then measure the bulb brightness

S4: Get a different battery, bulb and set of wires and build a second circuit with the battery in the opposite orientation.

S5: Using the same components, turn the battery in the opposite orientation.

Response S1 represents students that are using circular reasoning to connect a proposed experiment to the hypothesis. These students rely heavily on previously made observations, and struggle to invent new experiments. Response S2 represents students using the *non sequitur*, where they propose an actual experiment, but the experiment does not test the hypothesis. Response S3 represents students utilizing jargon that they have heard in class but that they either don't understand or don't articulate. Responses S4 and S5 represent students proposing different experiments that could lead to support or non-support of the hypothesis. We'll discuss the difference between S4 and S5 in the next chapter. For now, these two responses represent good thinking with respect to connecting the hypothesis to a useful testing experiment.

When completing this short activity in class as part of groups, almost all of the groups converged on a response similar to S4 and S5 fairly quickly. However, when we posed the question individually before instruction, we found that a surprisingly large percentage (~75%) of students responded like S1, S2, or S3 with the remaining students responding like S4 or S5. In group settings, it is possible that stronger students were driving the group without any explicit discussion about the reasoning process, and that the high student-to-faculty ratio made it difficult for direct instructor intervention to ensure these discussions took place.

The moral of this story is that you must be cautious with science thinking in your group discussions. The S1 students could easily recognize the superiority of the S4 or S5 arguments when they were presented in the group. However, these students struggled to *invent* such an experiment on their own. It is this invention that is the fundamental kernel of hypothetical-deductive thinking that we want to develop.

Thinking Task: If . . . And . . . Then . . .

Like we did in the previous chapters, we can use the educational and philosophical research we just discussed on hypothetical-deductive thinking to inform an approach to getting students to think about what it is they are doing when completing tasks requiring this thinking pattern. We want to build and use a support structure to get *all* students to start thinking and inventing hypothesis-experiment connections. We learned in Chapter 3 that student metacognition is the key to improvements in deployment of science thinking. We must get them to actively think about what they are thinking when engaged in science practice.

An effective way of scaffolding this process is by using the explicit construct of what Lawson calls the "If . . . and . . . then . . ." (IAT) statement (Moore, 2012; Lawson, A., 2000). Thinking Task 6.1 shows a general worksheet that can be used with any content that scaffolds the stages of the hypothetical-deductive method shown in Figure 6.1. In this way, hypothetical-deductive thinking is being made explicit, through discussion students are reflecting on their thinking, and the worksheets themselves can be assessed to make the thinking pattern count.

Thinking Task 6.1 Hypothetical-Deductive Thinking

Construct an "IF . . . AND . . . THEN . . ." statement in the following boxes:

Figure 6.2 "IF . . . AND . . . THEN . . ." worksheet

IF ...
AND ...
THEN ...
AND/BUT ...
THEREFORE ...

Source: Taken from Moore, 2017

Table 6.2 describes the basic construction of the IAT statement, which we describe and model for the students. The basic structure is as follows:

> IF a hypothesis,
> AND we do this experiment,
> THEN this would be the result,
> AND/BUT the actual result was this,
> THEREFORE *the hypothesis is supported/falsified.*

TABLE 6.2 MAKING HYPOTHETICAL-DEDUCTIVE THINKING FOR LIGHT REFLECTION EXPLICIT THROUGH THE IAT STATEMENT

If . . .	Hypothesis	Light reflects off a plane mirror at the same angle at which it strikes the mirror.
And . . .	Testing experiment	We aim a beam of light at an angle of 25° with respect to the mirror.
Then . . .	Result if hypothesis is true	The reflected beam will also be at an angle of 25° with respect to the mirror.
And/But . . .	Actual result of testing experiment	The beam did reflect at a 25° angle.
Therefore . . .	Conclusion	The hypothesis is supported.

By working with students to construct statements like this for their hypotheses and crazy ideas, we force them to do the following:

1. to explicitly state their hypothesis,
2. to articulate the testing experiment they intend to do,
3. to think about what prediction the hypothesis should lead to, and
4. to reflect on what the evidence tells them.

Let's look at a specific example. Go back and look at Activity 5.2 in the previous chapter, where students completed an observation experiment on light reflection. This observation experiment led the student to the hypothesis that light reflects off a plane mirror at the same angle at which it strikes the mirror, as shown in the student work pictured in Figure 5.10. How might we test this hypothesis? As one example, the student could assign an arbitrary incoming angle, preferably one for which they haven't yet made an observation, and then measure the reflected angle. For example, the hypothesis tells us that an incoming beam of light incident at an angle of 25° should reflect off of the mirror at an angle of 25°.

Table 6.2 describes the IAT statement the student would construct and document using Thinking Task 6.1. The statement would read as follows:

IF light reflects off a plane mirror at the same angle at which it strikes the mirror,

AND we aim a beam of light at an angle of 25° with respect to the mirror,

THEN the reflected beam will also be at an angle of 25° with respect to the mirror,

AND the beam did reflect at a 25° angle,
THEREFORE the hypothesis is supported.

The result is some really long run-on sentences, which is why Thinking Task 6.1 is nice to help structure the student's thinking.

How might we assess the thinking going on during this activity? Once again, I want to point you to the excellent work already done by the Rutgers University Physics Education Research Group. As I mentioned in the previous chapter, this group has developed a framework for teaching practice-based science that they call the Investigating Science Learning Environment (ISLE). They have several assessment tools and rubrics that they have been developed over the years that perfectly align with our goals of assessing hypothetical-deductive thinking. Table 6.3 shows example criteria for assessing hypothetical-deductive thinking taken from their larger rubric on testing experiments (Etkina, et al., 2006). I have pulled three criteria from their work corresponding to IF . . . AND . . . and THEN . . . components of Thinking Task 6.1. This demonstrates how you can develop your own rubrics.

TABLE 6.3 EXAMPLE CRITERIA FROM RUBRIC ON DESIGNING AND CONDUCTING TESTING EXPERIMENTS

Ability	Missing	Inadequate	Needs improvement	Adequate
IF . . . Is able to identify the hypothesis to be tested	No mention is made of a hypothesis.	An attempt is made to identify the hypothesis to be tested but is described in a confusing manner.	The hypothesis to be tested is described but there are minor omissions or vague details.	The hypothesis is clearly stated.
AND . . . Is able to design a reliable experiment that tests the hypothesis	The experiment does not test the hypothesis.	The experiment tests the hypothesis, but due to the nature of the design it is likely the data will lead to an incorrect judgment.	The experiment tests the hypothesis, but due to the nature of the design there is a moderate chance the data will lead to an inconclusive judgment.	The experiment tests the hypothesis and has a high likelihood of producing data that will lead to a conclusive judgment.
THEN . . . Is able to make a reasonable prediction based on a hypothesis	No attempt to make a prediction is made.	A prediction is made that is distinct from the hypothesis but is not based on it.	A prediction is made that follows from the hypothesis but does not incorporate assumptions.	A prediction is made that follows from the hypothesis and incorporates assumptions.

Source: From Etkina, et al., 2006

Similar to the example we looked at in Chapter 5, the larger rubric is designed to assess the science practice of designing and conducting experiments, and some of the individual criteria within that rubric center on the hypothetical-deductive process. This is a concrete example of what we were discussing in Chapter 2: successful execution of science practice *requires* good science thinking.

Does the Distance from the Sun Determine Seasons?

For another example of using Thinking Task 6.1 in your classroom, Activity 6.1 combines several science practices with the thinking pattern of hypothetical-deductive reasoning. Specifically, students test the widely held, but incorrect, belief that the change in seasons is a result of our distance from the sun. First, students have to decide what the hypothesis is based on a statement provided. This is more difficult than it seems. Then, students make a prediction about the Sun–Earth distance during various times of the year based on the hypothesis. The students must then decide how they will use the provided data to test the prediction. Finally, students analyze the data and make a judgement using argument from evidence.

Activity 6.1 What Causes the Seasons?

Part I: What's the Hypothesis?

Science Practice:

Ask questions and define problems

Hypothetical-Deductive Thinking:

During a particularly hot day, a group of students are discussing why it's hotter in the summer compared to the winter. One of the students makes the following statement:

I learned in my science class that the Earth moves in an elliptical orbit. That means that the Earth is closer to the sun sometimes during the year and further other times. It's hotter in the summer because the Earth is closer to the Sun during the summer months.

Using this student's thinking, write a short testable hypothesis about what causes the seasons.

Part II: Make a Prediction

Science Practice:

Obtain, evaluate, and communicate information

Hypothetical-Deductive Thinking:

What data could you obtain to test this hypothesis?
    What does the hypothesis predict?

Complete the first three boxes on the hypothetical-deductive thinking worksheet (Thinking Task 6.1).

Part III: Make a Judgement

Science Practice:

Analyze and interpret data, engage in argument from evidence

The following table shows the distance between the Earth and the Sun during January and July of 2018. The sun is at the "aphelion" when it is at its greatest distance and at the "perihelion" when it is at its closest distance during the year.

Date	Earth–Sun distance (miles)
January 2, 2018	91,401,983
July 6, 2018	94,507,803

In 2018, when was the sun at aphelion and when was it at perihelion?
    Was the Sun closest to the Earth in summer or winter?

Hypothetical-Deductive Thinking:

Complete the final two boxes on the hypothetical-deductive thinking worksheet (Thinking Task 6.1).

Figure 6.3 *Argument from Evidence* worksheet

Claim:

Evidence:	Reason:

Source: Taken from Moore, 2017

Make a claim about whether or not the Earth-Sun distance causes the seasons. Then, complete the *Argument from Evidence* worksheet (Figure 6.3).

In Part I, we provide a common student statement about the cause of the seasons. The contrived dialog states that summer is hot because the Earth is closest to the Sun. The hypothesis we want the students in class to come up with from that statement is that the seasons are caused by the Earth-Sun distance. This hypothesis is incorrect, as we will see. However, this idea is so common that even Harvard University graduates get seasons wrong 90% of the time (Paschka, 2018).

Even if you have explicitly discussed in class the causes of the seasons (tilt!), I can guarantee that most of your students will *still* believe the alternate Earth–Sun distance hypothesis. Some of you reading this right now might hold this idea. As I discussed earlier in this chapter, this incorrect idea really does have some validity, since it's certainly not obvious that the seasons would be caused by the Earth's tilt. In fact, based off of a child's past experiences (or an adult's), the idea that the Earth is warmer when it's closer to the giant fireball in the sky makes a whole lot of sense. We have a pretty simple model for hot stuff. As you get closer to big balls of fire you feel more heat. Remember the stove with the red glowing things we talked about in the Introduction and Chapter 1? You probably also remember that little picture of the Earth's elliptical orbit, where the Earth is closer to the sun during certain parts of the year? Naturally, you assume the hot summer comes when the Earth is closer to the big ball of fire.

The point here is that it's an idea that is just as good as any other idea until we have data that either supports it or falsifies it. That's what this chapter has been all about: coming up with some ideas and then testing those ideas. At the beginning of Activity 6.1, your students have a pretty strong likelihood of believing the hypothesis they form in Part I. That's perfectly acceptable, since they are going to test it, and then form their own arguments based on the data for why it's wrong, as opposed to "learning" by being told.

In Part II, students think about the types of data that could support or falsify the hypothesis. You will want to coach your students through the science practice of obtaining, evaluating, and communicating scientific information, such that they decide that data for the distance between the Earth and the Sun could support their idea. The prediction that the hypothesis makes is that the Earth will be closer to the Sun in July, and further from the Sun in January. (Unless you live in the southern hemisphere, where this activity will not work as well.)

Finally, in Part III, students evaluate and interpret the data that was provided to them. You could also have the students find this data on their own if you have access to the appropriate resources in your classroom. (I actually prefer that students find their own data. I only presented data in Activity 6.1 in an effort to make the writing clearer.) After evaluating the data, the students formally complete an IAT statement using the Thinking Task 6.1 worksheet. Figure 6.3 shows the *Argument from Evidence* worksheet that I discuss in more detail in Chapter 6 of my other book *Creating Scientists* (Moore, 2017).

By completing this worksheet, the student is forced to make a prediction using their hypothesis. In this particular case, the prediction that they chose does not match with the reality that they then observe. Since the student has built their own chain of reasoning, as opposed to just being told, then they are much more likely to become convinced and have their deeply set ideas evolve towards known, correct ideas.

Notice that this activity doesn't actually teach why the seasons happen. It only teaches what factor isn't the cause. However, since we know that students have a strongly held conception about the seasons that isn't accurate, it is imperative that we get them to dispatch with the incorrect hypothesis before moving on to constructing the real cause. In a sense, hypothetical-deductive thinking and testing experiments are perfect vessels for confronting student misconceptions.

Summary

In summary, I described the science thinking pattern called hypothetical-deductive reasoning, which is what goes on in the scientist mind as they think about what their hypotheses and models are trying to tell them about the world. We started by examining the types of experiments scientists do, such as observation, testing, and application experiments. We used the research on the teaching and learning of hypothetical-deductive thinking and the *explicit-reflective-count* framework from Chapter 3 to inform a practical "Thinking Task" worksheet that can be incorporated into any lesson where this thinking pattern is used. To illustrate how to use the worksheet, we looked at three examples, one on electric circuits, one on light reflection, and the other on astronomy and seasons.

The following is a brief summary of the main points:

◆ Experiments can be grouped based on the goals of the experimenter, which can be one of the following:

  ◇ generate new ideas,
  ◇ test proposed ideas, and
  ◇ solve a practical problem.

◆ These goals correspond to the following experiment types:

  ◇ observation experiments,
  ◇ testing experiments, and
  ◇ application experiments.

◆ The hypothetical-deductive process has the following five stages:

  ◇ The student forms many hypotheses through the hypothesis-generation process, or
  ◇ conceptions based on previous experiences.
  ◇ The student chooses a specific hypothesis to be tested.
  ◇ The student uses the hypothesis to make a previously unobserved prediction.
  ◇ The student uses the science practice of planning and conducting an experiment to check whether the prediction comes true.
  ◇ From the results, the student evaluates whether the hypothesis is supported or not.

◆ Students often have multiple competing ideas and/or "alternate" conceptions that are counter to known science. Testing experiments are excellent opportunities for students to test their ideas and convince themselves whether or not they are correct.

◆ Students struggle to invent good experiments that can test their hypotheses, often using one of the following incorrect approaches:

◇ circular reasoning, where student rely heavily on previously made observations;

◇ *non sequitur*, where they propose an actual experiment, but the experiment does not test the hypothesis; and

◇ jargon, where no experiment is proposed but jargon words are used to make it seem like one has.

◆ "If . . . And . . . Then" statements structure students thinking and have the following form:

◇ IF a hypothesis, AND we do this experiment, THEN this would be the result. AND/BUT the actual result was this, THEREFORE the hypothesis is supported/falsified.

◇ Constructing these statements forces student to do the following:

○ explicitly state their hypothesis,
○ articulate the testing experiment they intend to do,
○ think about what prediction the hypothesis should lead to, and
○ reflect on what the evidence tells them.

References

Borke, H. (1975). Piaget's Mountains Revisited: Changes in the Egocentric Landscape. *Developmental Psychology, 11*(2), 240–243.

Coletta, V. P., & Phillips, J. A. (2005). Interpreting FCI scores: Normalized gain, preinstruction scores, and scientific reasoning ability. *American Journal of Physics, 73*, 1172.

Danner, F., & Day, M. (1977). Eliciting Formal Operations. *Child Development, 48*(4).

Etkina, E., Van Heuvelen, A., Brookes, D., & Mills, D. (2002). Role of Experiments in Physics Instruction – A Process Approach. *The Physics Teacher, 40*.

Etkina, E., Van Heuvelen, A., White-Brahmia, S., Brookes, D., Gentile, M., Murthy, S., . . . Warren, A. (2006). Scientific abilities and their assessment. *Physical Review ST Physics Education Research, 2*, 020103.

Feynman, R. (1965). *The Character of Physical Law.* Modern Library.

Godfrey-Smith, P. (2003). *Theory and Reality: An Introduction to the Philosophy of Science.* Chicago: University of Chicago Press.

Inhelder, B., & Piaget, J. (1969). *Early Growth of Logic in the Child.* New York, NY: W. W. Norton & Company, Inc.

Kuhn, D. (2004). In U. Goswami (ed.), *Blackwell Handbook of Childhood Cognitive Development* (pp. 371–393). Malden, MA: Wiley-Blackwell.

Latour, B. (1987). *Science in Action: How to Follow Scientists and Engineers through Society.* Milton Keynes, UK: Open University Press.

Lawson, A. (2000). The Generality of Hypothetico-Deductive Reasoning: Making Scientific Thinking Explicit. *The American Biology Teacher, 62*(7), 482–495.

Lawson, A. E., Clark, B., Cramer-Meldrum, E., Falconer, K. A., Sequist, J., & Kwon, Y. (2000). Development of scientific reasoning in college biology: Do two levels of general hypothesis-testing skills exist? *Journal of Research on Science Teaching, 37,* 81.

Lawson, A., Alkhoury, S., Benford, R., Clark, B., & Falconer, K. (2000). What kinds of scientific concepts exist? Concept construction and intellectual development in college biology. *Journal of Research in Science Teaching, 37,* 996.

Moore, C. (2017). *Creating Scientists: Teaching and Assessing Science Practice for the NGSS.* New York, NY: Routledge.

Moore, J. C. (2012). Transitional to Formal Operational: Using Authentic Research Experiences to Get Non-Science Students to Think More Like Scientists. *European Journal of Physics Education, 3*(4), 1–12.

Moore, J. C., & Rubbo, L. J. (2012). Scientific reasoning abilities of nonscience majors in physics-based courses. *Physical Review Special Topics – Physics Education Research, 8,* 010106.

Paschka, L. (2018, June 22). *Harvard Graduates Explain Seasons.* Retrieved from TEDEd: https://ed.ted.com/on/xKxsSA5w

7

What Does This Evidence Tell Me, and Do I Believe It?

"How we choose our 'authorities' and place a value on such information, is just another skill rarely taught in our education systems. It's little wonder that to most folk, sound bites and talking heads are enough to count as experts. . . . Educators themselves have to be prepared to show that 'evidence' and 'answers' are two separate things by firmly believing that, themselves."

—Australian teacher Mike McRae (McRae, 2006)

Metacognition is an awareness and understanding of your thought processes. So far in this book, we have approached metacognition from an educational standpoint. That is to say, we have discussed how getting students to reflect on what they are learning, doing, and thinking is critical for the development of understanding. As I have repeated over and over throughout the book, student metacognition is the key to improvements in deployment of science thinking, where the learning of science requires students to think about all of these great thinking patterns. To this end, I have provided multiple "Thinking Tasks" in previous chapters and I have shown you examples of how to use them in your classroom. These tasks are all examples of metacognitive activities that are designed to force student reflection on their own thoughts.

However, metacognition is also a science thinking pattern in itself that is used by expert scientists as they practice. Scientists *critically* examine their own knowledge, methods, and reasoning, as well as the evidence and arguments of others. For example, when making judgements the scientist recognizes that all measurements in science come with some degree of uncertainty. We can measure the length of a string using a ruler and get a pretty good estimate of its length. However, the ruler itself has some limitations, such as the spacing between the markings. We can still learn a lot about the string length, but there is always some uncertainty.

Good science thinking incorporates this uncertainty in the evaluation of the *relative value of evidence*. A good scientist can make a judgement using the results of some experiment, but can maintain a sense of skepticism and a variable amount of confidence in their judgement based on the degree to which they think they know something. This variable confidence requires really strong metacognitive faculties, since it requires a constant reflection on not just the knowledge, but all of the process and thinking that went into discovering the knowledge. Basically, great scientists walk around always thinking they're wrong, at least at some level. Surprisingly, that takes a whole lot more confidence than the reverse!

This chapter is devoted to getting your students to *critically* evaluate their own thinking, their own judgements, and the thinking and judgements of others. Specifically, we will discuss the philosophical foundation of metacognition and human cognitive development's role in shaping how it's used. We will break metacognition into two areas:

1. knowing what you're thinking, and
2. controlling what you're thinking.

Within the realm of "knowing," we will discuss how to get students to think about the relative value of evidence within science, and re-examine the testing experiments from the previous chapter to better understand our "not-wrong" formulation and the nature of "proof" in science. With respect to "controlling," we will discuss teaching students how to direct their own learning. All of this background will inform a final set of Thinking Tasks that you can use in your classroom to help ensure students are truly reflecting on their lessons and the level of certainty their results can provide. Finally, I will show you how to use the Thinking Tasks through several examples. We will look back at several example activities already discussed in previous chapters and see how to improve them even further by incorporating metacognitive questioning.

Metacognition

In the late 70s, Psychologist John Flavell coined the term "metacognition," which generally means "thinking about thinking" (Flavell, 1979). However, philosophers and psychologists have been concerned with the mental processes that happen as we think since as far back as Aristotle. Education theorist John Dewey considered reflection to be one of the central components of learning at the beginning of the last century, with publication of his book *How We Think* (Dewey, 1910).

As detailed in Table 7.1, metacognition can be broken into two categories as follows (Flavell, 1979):

1. metacognitive awareness, and
2. metacognitive regulation.

Metacognitive awareness generally refers to thinking about what we know, the ways of knowing, and connecting the two. Metacognitive regulation refers to the process of directing our learning. We can think of these two categories as a student knowing what and how they're thinking, and being able to direct their own thinking, respectively.

Metacognitive awareness can be broken down into three different types as follows and as detailed in Table 7.2:

1. declarative awareness,
2. procedural awareness, and
3. conditional awareness.

TABLE 7.1 THE TWO CATEGORIES OF METACOGNITION

Category	Description
Metacognitive awareness	The awareness of one's thinking processes.
Metacognitive regulation	The ability to manage and direct of one's thinking.

Source: Flavell, 1979

TABLE 7.2 THE THREE TYPES OF METACOGNITIVE AWARENESS

Metacognitive awareness	Description
Declarative	Being aware of what we know, what we don't know, and what we want to know.
Procedural	Being aware of approaches and strategies to learning.
Conditional	Knowing how to combine declarative and procedural awareness to direct the completion of tasks.

Source: Flavell, 1979

Declarative awareness refers to a student being aware of what they know, what they don't know, and what they want to know. For example, the student might recognize that they know "the mitochondria is the powerhouse of the cell." Good declarative awareness would mean that they can recognize that they don't know why it is a "powerhouse" or what "powerhouse" means. In Chapter 4 we talked about patterns and recognizing relationships in quantitative data. The student might see a well-definable relationship emerge, but still be aware that they don't have an explanation and that they need one.

Procedural awareness refers to a student's understanding of the different procedures and approaches to gaining knowledge. This book and my previous book, *Creating Scientists*, are about helping students develop procedural awareness by explicitly teaching science practices and science thinking within your classroom. For example, it the student wants to know how light reflects off of a plane mirror, then they have to be aware of the scientific procedure to accomplish that learning: planning and conducting an observation experiment and the associated thinking patterns.

Conditional awareness refers to the student's understanding of how and when to deploy thinking strategies. Again, the student may recognize that they don't know how light reflects off of a mirror (declarative awareness), and they may have learned about observation experiments in general or in another context (procedural awareness). Conditional awareness refers to the student being able to decide that the observation experiment could lead them to the knowledge they want. They are aware that they have the mental means to complete the task. Note that many different strategies could be used, such as referring to a book or asking their friend what they know about reflection. In fact, a good metacognitive strategy is to think about all of the different ways procedural and declarative awareness can lead to knowledge.

Metacognitive awareness can be considered a type of "thinking-in-action," where the student thinks about the thinking they have done, what they know, or the activities they could or did do while meaningfully engaged in the activity. Metacognitive regulation would be best described as "thinking-on-action," where the student thinks about how to direct their learning. Table 7.3 details the three abilities that are essential to metacognitive regulation. These three abilities are as follows:

1. planning,
2. monitoring, and
3. evaluating.

Planning includes identifying the problem, choosing various strategies, organizing thoughts, and possibly predicting outcomes. For example, the IAT statements from Thinking Task 6.1 structure metacognitive planning with respect to testing experiments. Monitoring involves actively thinking about thinking and strategies in the process of completing tasks. It includes the testing and revising of strategies and thinking. For example, Thinking Tasks 4.1 on pattern recognition is a set of questions deployed during a task to get students to monitor their thinking during that task. Finally, evaluating thinking means checking outcomes against some specific criteria of effectiveness. Note that in order to do metacognitive regulation well, students also need metacognitive awareness.

As I mentioned in the introduction to this chapter, we can look at metacognition from an educational perspective and from a science thinking perspective. Within the educational perspective, we use the research on metacognition with respect to student learning to guide the development and implementation of science lessons. This is the student thinking about thinking in the process of learning science. Within the science thinking perspective, we want to know how the expert scientist thinks about their own thinking in the process of doing science. We use the educational

TABLE 7.3 THE THREE ABILITIES ESSENTIAL TO METACOGNITIVE REGULATION

Metacognitive regulation	Description
Planning	Selection of strategies to complete the task.
Monitoring	Awareness of performance during the task.
Evaluating	Evaluation of the outcome of the task and strategies used.

Source: Flavell, 1979

perspective to help us teach the student to work within the science thinking perspective.

Metacognition in Science Education

Let's look at how cognitive and education science has linked metacognition to how students learn. As our understanding of how we learn has
progressed over the last few decades, we've begun to recognize the massive role metacognition plays. In fact, metacognitive ability appears to be
the defining distinguisher between expert thinkers and novices. Expert
thinkers know how to recognize flaws in their thinking, they can articulate
their thinking process, and they have the confidence to revise their thinking when warranted (Brown, et al., 1983). The expert scientist consistently
evaluates their own thinking and utilizes multiple resources towards solving a problem, making an observation, coming up with a hypothesis, and
conducting experiments. The novice is typically "stuck" in one type of
framing and rarely evaluates their own thinking (Edmondson & Novak,
1993).

As an adult educator, you actually engage these types of metacognitive
abilities every day. For example, when developing a lesson plan, you
decide on what methods to use, the learning progression, and you think
about how students might approach the content. You try to recognize
where students might have the most difficulty, and if you don't know, you
seek out help. You use the experience gained from conducting the lesson
to inform future teaching moves, and seek out guidance (like this book!)
to learn more. You use metacognitive abilities to help decide what you
understand and what you don't understand. In short, you direct your own
learning. Your students often lack these abilities, and if they know about
them, the often don't know when to use them (Flavell & Wellman, 1977).

The role of metacognition in human development was described by
both Jean Piaget and Lev Vygotsky in their competing theories of human
development. Specifically, Piaget described a child's "consciousness of
cognizance" as the point where they could articulate the processes they
used to complete a task (Inhelder & Piaget, 1969). According to Piaget,
this ability forms around the age of seven. Vygotsky termed a similar
process as the use of the child's "inner speech," where they articulate their
internal thoughts during sense-making (Vygotsky, 1986). Both of these
ideas fit well with what we now call metacognition.

Not surprisingly, metacognitive abilities develop over time, with some fundamental knowledge being necessary for their use (Brown & DeLoache, 1978). For example, with no knowledge of the concept of energy, the student would have an exceedingly difficult time directing their learning about the topic, or even examining their thinking about energy. At an even more basic level, an understanding of something as simple as counting requires some foundational knowledge.

In the last chapter, we discussed the distinction between concrete, hypothetical, and theoretical concepts, where a student's ability to understand abstract science content depends on their developmental level (Lawson, et al., 2000; Coletta & Phillips, 2005; Moore, 2012; Moore & Rubbo, 2012). With small children, we try to use concrete experiences, such as having them play with two balls and then giving them a third while asking them to talk about how they know how many balls they have. This progression through content types allows for the practical development of metacognition.

What's really important from this discussion, though, is that you should be starting to see how all of this leads to the integration of knowing, doing, and thinking necessary for understanding. A student can't think about their own thinking with respect to some concept without knowing about that concept. However, to really understand the concept, they have to think about it and do something with it. The research on student metacognition during the learning process is one of the key foundations on which situated cognition was based, and therefore the foundation of the *knowing-doing-thinking* theory of understanding on which this book is based (Brown, et al., 1989).

You should notice by now that the Thinking Tasks that I have presented throughout the book are designed to be metacognitive awareness activities. We are trying to teach students how the scientist thinks when they complete certain tasks: how do they plan, how do they monitor their own thinking, and how do they evaluate their thinking? Of course, to do this, students need awareness of metacognition. This is why we combine explicit instruction of science thinking patterns and science practices (metacognitive awareness) with the opportunity to use and reflect on them independently (metacognitive regulation), which makes up the first two parts of the *explicit-reflective-count* framework described in Chapter 3.

I have chosen metacognition to be the focus of the last chapter within Part II of this book because metacognition is the most fundamental thinking task your students can do. In this section, I really wanted to highlight the why and how behind the Thinking Tasks throughout the rest of the book. It is these thinking tasks that take your teaching from simple inquiry to apprenticeship.

Relative Value of Evidence

Now, let's look at how the scientist uses metacognition in the process of doing science. Specifically, we're going to discuss how the student's and scientist's view of science informs their thinking-on-action and thinking-in-action. We'll then look at an important concept within the scientific community called the "relative value of evidence."

Table 7.4 shows a selection from the taxonomy of student and scientist views about science that we discussed in Chapter 1 (Hestenes & Halloun, 1998). For metacognition, we are interested in the dimensions of validity and reflective thinking, since how a person views the practice of science is fundamentally a function of their epistemological beliefs (Edmondson & Novak, 1993). That is to say, a person's belief about what it takes to know stuff informs how they think during that process of knowing.

The typical scientist views science as tentative and a process, which contrasts with the student belief that science is a collection of facts to commit to memory. Let's start by looking at how the student view might affect their metacognitive strategies. For example, a student might actually have very strong metacognitive abilities. However, if they are seeking "facts," then their evaluation of their learning during metacognitive regulation may lead them to (rightfully) judge good inquiry-based learning activities as inefficient. After all, it takes a lot less time to just tell a fact. These students are often very bright, so committing facts to memory is relatively easy. They see the hands-on, inquiry-based activity as a means

TABLE 7.4 A SELECTION FROM THE TAXONOMY OF STUDENT AND SCIENTIST VIEWS ABOUT SCIENCE

Dimension	How students view science	How scientists view science
Validity	Scientific knowledge is exact, absolute, and final.	Scientific knowledge is tentative and refutable.
Reflective thinking	For meaningful understanding of science, one needs to memorize facts.	Science is a process that allows for the recognition of patterns.

Source: Adapted from Hestenes & Halloun, 1998

to help "other" students learn and remember the fact, but inefficient for themselves personally. In fact, we've found that the students that are best at thinking about thinking are often the most frustrated with inquiry-based lessons when no explicit science thinking metacognitive tasks are assigned.

Let's carry this forward. Their view is that the end goal is the learning of facts, so they are completely blind to the idea that knowledge can be tentative and refutable, which is a view strongly held by scientists. This means that some of your best students will have difficulty evaluating uncertainty in measurements and understanding what uncertainty even means, resorting to the notorious "human error" explanation for all variations from "knowns." They are also the first to be frustrated when they find out something they "learned" is not quite right or complete.

On the other hand, the scientist recognizes that all measurements in science come with some degree of uncertainty when they make judgements. For example, we can measure the length of a string using a ruler and get a pretty good estimate of its length. However, the ruler itself has some limitations, such as the spacing between the markings. The string could also have some elasticity, which means its length could vary slightly with the amount of force being applied to it. We can still learn a lot about the string length, but there is always some uncertainty. Good science thinking incorporates this uncertainty in the evaluation of evidence. A good scientist can make a judgement using the results of some experiment, but can maintain a sense of skepticism and a variable amount of confidence in their judgement based on the degree to which they know something.

This variable confidence in data is what we call an evaluation of the "relative value of evidence." Some evidence is more valuable than other evidence, and the scientist must engage in a metacognitive process of evaluating the relative value of evidence when building an argument from evidence, as one example. The entire concept of variability in value relies on the epistemological belief that knowledge is tentative and refutable. "Facts" seem to change as we make more measurements, create better explanations, or a combination of both.

Figure 7.1 shows a simple example of variable evidence value, where two crudely drawn stick-people are trying to measure the length of a doorway to see if a specific door will fit. One person uses a piece of string and discovers the door to be about 2.5 string-lengths. They also measure the doorway to be about 2.5 string-lengths, so they conclude that the door should fit. The other person uses a measuring tape and finds the door to

Figure 7.1 Sketch of two approaches to measurement: (a) string length, and (b) tape measure in meters

be about 2.1 meters. The doorway is found to be about 2.0 meters, so they conclude that the door will not fit.

In this situation, we have two arguments backed by evidence. In both cases, the evidence seems to support the argument. However, in the second case we can clearly determine that the value of the evidence is greater than in the first case. Why? Because the precision of the measurement is greater, and therefore potentially more reliable. Of course, there is still some uncertainty in the tape measure result, since we can only measure to the nearest centimeter. There also could be some systematic error resulting from an improperly printed tape measure, for example. The scientists employing good metacognition would think about all of this when evaluating the evidence.

The relative value of evidence doesn't just concern measurement uncertainty, but also an evaluation of assumptions that we and others make. For example, let's review the testing experiments and hypothetical-deductive process from Chapter 6. During that process, a student makes a judgement based on evidence concerning the validity of the hypothesis. It's easy to think that a contradictory result with respect to the prediction means the hypothesis is completely invalid, or that a result that is in line with the prediction means the hypothesis is proven. However, scientists don't use words like "proven" for good reason. We are always making assumptions, and those assumptions themselves lead to variable uncertainty.

For example, confirming the predictions of a hypothesis does not *prove* conclusively that the hypothesis is correct, but merely increases the probability that it is correct. To illustrate, look at the following IAT statement concerning the orientation of a battery activity from Chapter 6:

IF the orientation of the battery doesn't affect the circuit,
AND we build another circuit with the battery in the opposite direction,
THEN the bulbs in both circuits will be the same brightness.
AND the bulbs were the same brightness,
THEREFORE the hypothesis is supported.

The fact that the bulbs ended up being the same brightness does *support* the hypothesis, but it does not *prove* the hypothesis. Since we built two different circuits, it's possible that components of the circuits are not identical, such as the bulbs, wires, or batteries themselves. The battery direction *might* matter, but it seems like it doesn't because we have different bulb specifications. We are assuming that everything in the circuit is identical, and this assumption itself might not be true. It's also possible that orientation doesn't matter when it comes to bulbs, but could matter with other types of electrical components. Therefore, we have a limit to what we can tell from this experiment alone: it appears the orientation doesn't matter when connected to bulbs. Maybe.

Similarly, a result that is contrary to the prediction does not necessarily mean that the hypothesis is falsified. Imagine your phone stops working. You hypothesize that the battery has died. Based on this hypothesis, you plug your phone into a charger and walk away. The testing experiment here is to charge the phone, with the hypothesis predicting that doing so will make the phone work again. Later, you come back to your phone and it still doesn't work. Have we falsified the hypothesis that the batteries are dead? Not necessarily, because everything we have done has been based on the assumption that the charger works. The battery could be fine and something else could be wrong with the phone, or the battery could actually be dead and the charger just didn't work.

Note that a healthy questioning of certainty in measurements and assumptions doesn't mean that we can never know anything. It just means that there are limits to what we can extrapolate from an experiment or set of experiments, and it is the scientist's job to make sure those limits are understood. It also suggests that the scientist (and science student) needs to accept a large degree of openness to ideas.

The scientist must think deeply about the uncertainties that exist in measurements and all of the possible assumptions that they are making when doing science. This requires metacognitive awareness and regulation. The combination of their declarative and procedural awareness with constant monitoring and evaluation of the relative value of what they think they know and their assumptions yields a very powerful skepticism. This skepticism about everything, even their own ideas, is the hallmark of the successful scientist. If you want your students to be good scientific thinkers, then you must train them to be skeptical thinkers that constantly question the methods, results, and logic of others and themselves.

Thinking Tasks: Metacognition

As discussed, the Thinking Tasks from the previous chapters are all examples of metacognitive tasks designed to improve student metacognitive awareness through explicit and reflective focus on the thinking patterns during scaffolded activities. Once this metacognitive awareness is established, students can start to direct their own thinking during explorations, where they have freedom to ask their own questions and completely design their own investigations. Thinking Task 7.1 is a worksheet you can use during these explorations to guide your students through metacognitive regulation.

Thinking Task 7.1 Thinking About Doing

Part I: Planning

Which science practices will you use to complete the task?
Which science thinking patterns will you use during the completion of the task?

Part II: Monitoring

Describe what's going on in your mind while you complete this task.

Did you make any revisions to the plan while completing the task?

Part III: Evaluating

Did the practices and thinking that you did during the task lead to a good result?
Are you not sure about anything that you did? Explain.

So far in this book, we haven't discussed in great detail exploration, which is the final principle method of cognitive apprenticeship as shown in Table 3.1. In an exploration activity, students investigate new methods, strategies, and test new hypotheses by exploring a problem. Students can set their own goals and develop their own testing strategies, all of which fosters independent learning. My previous book *Creating Scientists* spent an entire chapter detailing best practices for capstone explorations, and I encourage you to read it (Moore, 2017). I'll show you an example of using Thinking Task 7.1 in a capstone exploration in the next chapter.

In this chapter, I'm going to focus on metacognition from the perspective of science thinking in the practice of science, and specifically the relative value of evidence. Like we did in the previous chapters, we can use the educational and philosophical research we just discussed on the metacognition of the scientist to inform the construction of a structure that supports students developing this ability. In particular, we want students to begin analyzing the relative value of evidence with respect the measurements that they make and their assumptions-based judgements.

Thinking Task 7.2 shows a short series of questions that you can insert into any lesson that involves a measurement. Thinking Task 7.3 shows a short series of questions that you can insert into any lesson that involves making a judgement. Both of these tasks can be done as either a separate worksheet, the questions can be inserted into an existing worksheet, or you can simply ask these questions during the completion of the activity. As you will see in the example activities later in this chapter, you can also edit these questions to better fit your specific content.

Thinking Task 7.2   Thinking About Uncertainty

What are you trying to measure?
  What methods could you use to make the measurement?
  What are the limitations of those measurement methods?
  How certain are you in your measurement?

Thinking Task 7.3   Thinking About Assumptions

When completing the task, did you make any assumptions?
  If those assumptions were not true, would it affect your judgement?
  How reliable are the methods you used? Why?
  How confident are you in the judgement that you made? Why?

Each of these tasks is informed by the concept of metacognitive awareness. The questions in Thinking Task 7.2 are designed to get students to evaluate what they think they know, the methods of measurement that can be used, the limits of certainty those methods produce, and how these combine to form a reasonable estimate of uncertainty. The questions in Thinking Task 7.3 are designed to get students to think about their assumptions, the reliability of their methods, and how these combine to form a reasonable estimate of confidence in a judgement.

Measuring Light Reflection

In Chapter 5 we looked at an example activity on light reflection that demonstrated the use of control of variables thinking in the classroom. This activity was motivated by the following NGSS performance expectations:

4-PS4–2.   Students who demonstrate understanding can *develop a model* to describe that light reflecting from objects and entering the eye allows objects to be seen.

We're now going to slightly modify this activity to explicitly incorporate active and explicit thinking about the relative value of evidence. Activity 7.1 is a slightly modified version of Activity 5.2, with the addition of metacognitive questioning detailed in Thinking Task 7.2.

Activity 7.1 Ray Model of Light and Reflection

Part I: Observing Reflection Off a Plane Mirror

Science Practice:

Asking questions and making observations

Your group is going to build and use a simple device that makes a beam of light. This beam of light will allow your group to investigate light reflection. Figure 7.2 shows the device. It is made up of a flashlight and a piece of cardboard with a narrow slit. Build this device with the materials you have been given. Make sure it produces a very thin beam of light. (Note to teacher: you may wish to construct the cardboard pieces beforehand.)

Aim the beam of light at the mirror and observe what happens. First, aim the beam directly at the mirror. Next, turn the mirror and observe what happens to the beam of light. Each member of your group should take a turn playing with the mirror and light beam.

Document your observations in your scientific notebook using both pictures and words. As a group, write one or two sentences that explains what you have observed.

Control of Variables:

From your observation, if you wanted to learn more about how reflected light behaves, what variable(s) might be relevant?

Figure 7.2 Schematic diagram of the lightbulb "ray" box

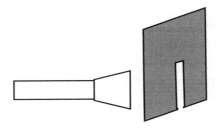

Relative Value of Evidence:

What are you trying to measure?
    What methods could you use to make the measurement?
    What are the limitations of those measurement methods?
    How certain are you in your measurement?
    Specifically, what changes do you notice in the beam as it goes through space? Could these changes cause problems with your measurement?

After completing this part wait for further instruction from the teacher before moving to the next part. One representative from your group will present to the class during a class conference.

Part II: An Observation Experiment for Reflection off Mirrors

Science Practice:

Planning and conducting investigations/developing and using models

Design and conduct an experiment that compares the incoming angle of a beam of light to the angle the reflected beam makes with a mirror.
Control of Variables:

What variable will you control (independent variable)?
    Which variable will you measure (dependent variable)?

Document the experiment in your science notebook. Summarize your results using a table.
Relative Value of Evidence:
Come up with a reasonable estimate of the uncertainty in the measurements that you made based on your thinking in the previous part.
Pattern Recognition:

Do you notice any patterns in the data?
    Can you come up with a model that you could use to predict future behavior?

In Part I, students construct a simple device that produces a thin beam of light, approximating a light "ray." They then aim the light beam at a plane mirror and sketch the resulting reflection for several different orientations of the mirror. Ultimately, they will conduct a formal observation experiment to discover the relationship between the incoming angle and the outgoing angle, as described in more detail in Chapter 5. The slight modifications I have made are the explicit incorporation of Thinking Task 7.2, where they are asked to think about the measurements that they are making and the limitations of those measurements. Again, these questions can be inserted directly into the worksheet, as shown in Activity 7.1, or used as verbal discussion questions during class.

There are two major components that contribute to uncertainty in the angle measurements the student can make:

1. beam spreading, and
2. instrument limitations.

Figure 7.3 shows a picture of the lightbulb box producing a "ray" that is then reflected off of a plane mirror. Notice how the beam size spreads as it moves through space to the point where it has a width of nearly a

Figure 7.3 Picture of a light "ray" from the lightbulb box reflecting off of a plane mirror. Notice how the beam diverges, creating uncertainty in the angle measurement

centimeter. You will have to guide the student to think about how this might affect the measurement. First, the student must decide what part of the beam to use. Should they trace a line down the center? Down one side? If down the center, then how should they define the center and how well can they measure that? If down a side, then what do they do at the intersection where the beam hits the mirror?

The students will probably use protractors to measure angles. You will have to guide the student to think about the accuracy of the measurement they can make with a protractor. How accurate is a protractor? How straight are the traced lines they created, and does that matter? Most protractors have markings every one degree. Without a marking between every degree, is it really possible to know the angle to within half a degree? Does the thickness of the traced line cause any measurement uncertainty?

Figure 7.4 shows an image of student work in their scientific notebook. Notice that the student has organized their results in a table. If the student

Figure 7.4 Sample student work showing the planning and results of a formal observation experiment. The angle the incoming beam makes with the mirror is found to be equal to the angle the outgoing beam makes with the mirror

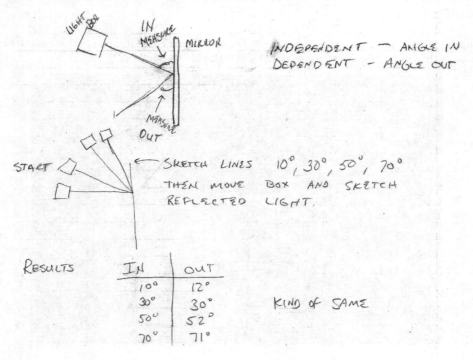

had not thought about measurement uncertainty beforehand, then they would be likely to view the 10° and 12° measurements as significantly different. This would result in significant difficulty recognizing a pattern.

Table 7.5 shows the same data from Figure 7.4 with the quantitative estimates of the uncertainty. When working through the Thinking Task, students can come up with a pretty good guess that they know the angle to within a couple of degrees. They can only make measurements with the protractor to within one degree, and the beam spreading and tracing issues possibly contribute another one degree of uncertainty. Now, the pattern is much clearer, since 10±2° is the same as 12±2°.

The act of thinking about all of these questions is a metacognitive task. Specifically, the student is thinking about the value of the evidence they are gathering. It goes deeper than that, though, since they are also forced to consider their measurement strategies in gory detail in the moment, instead of afterwards. This results in greater care being taken when making measurements.

It's also important to note here that the main point of the Thinking Task is not to guide students to some specific value for the uncertainty in the measurement angle, such as plus-or-minus two degrees. How to estimate uncertainty is a skill to develop over time, and one that can sometimes be pedagogically, developmentally, and field dependent. In the elementary grades we might think about uncertainty qualitatively. In the middle grades, uncertainty estimates will become quantitative but more akin to educated guessing. In high school, students should be learning more sophisticated methods of estimating uncertainty that can depend on the field and type of measurement being made. This chapter isn't about the specifics of estimating uncertainty, but about getting the student to think about where uncertainty comes from and to think deeper about the types of measurements that they are making.

TABLE 7.5 TABLE OF EXPERIMENTAL VALUES FROM FIGURE 7.4 WITH REASONABLE ESTIMATES OF UNCERTAINTY

Angle in	Angle out
10±2°	12±2°
30±2°	30±2°
50±2°	52±2°
71±2°	71±2°

TABLE 7.6 EXAMPLE CRITERION FOR ASSESSING RECOGNITION OF MEASUREMENT UNCERTAINTY

Ability	Missing	Inadequate	Needs improvement	Adequate
Is able to identify measurement uncertainties	No measurement uncertainties are identified.	Most measurement uncertainties are not identified.	Most measurement uncertainties are identified.	All measurement uncertainties are identified.

Anytime a measurement is being made students should be made to think about the relative value of the evidence that they are obtaining and how it could influence their judgements. In this way, we are making this thinking pattern explicit and reflective. To make it count, then you need to assess their ability to identify measurement uncertainty and how it can affect a judgement. Table 7.6 shows an example criterion for assessing a student's ability to identify measurement uncertainty. This criterion can be added to any rubric used to assess an activity.

Flipping Batteries

Now, let's look at an activity that gets students to critically analyze their assumptions and methods, and gets them to think about how assumptions can significantly affect judgements. Activity 7.2 is based on the same battery orientation experiment we've discussed in Chapter 6 and earlier in this chapter.

Activity 7.2   Flipping Batteries

Part I: Testing a Hypothesis

Science Practice:

Design and conduct an investigation

Hypothetical-Deductive Thinking:
Using the materials provided, build a single bulb circuit consisting of a battery, two wires and a bulb arranged such that the bulb is lit. Leave the completed circuit in the middle of your group's table as you complete the rest of this activity.

Imagine a student makes the following statement: "It doesn't matter which way the '+' sign on the battery is oriented. The circuit will work the same either way."

Complete an "If . . . And . . . Then . . ." worksheet for the student's hypothesis. Specifically, in your group identify the hypothesis to be tested, the testing experiment you would do, and the predicted result of that experiment if the hypothesis is true. DO NOT PERFORM THE EXPERIMENT!

Part II: Thinking About Assumptions

Metacognition:

Answer all of the following questions before moving to the next part:

Did you make any assumptions when designing your testing experiment?

If those assumptions turned out to not be true, how would it potentially affect the prediction?

We will now hold a scientific conference. Be prepared to discuss your group's ideas with the rest of the class. Do not move to the next section until the conference has concluded.

Part III: Testing the Hypothesis and Making a Judgement

Your group has been provided another set of materials. One option for testing the hypothesis is to build a new circuit, but this circuit should have the battery oriented in the opposite direction from the first circuit. Build the second circuit using the provided materials.

Was the result what you predicted?

Make a judgement about the hypothesis based on the results of the testing experiment.

How confident are you in the judgement that you made? Why?

We will now hold a scientific conference. Be prepared to discuss your group's results with the rest of the class. Do not move to the next section until the conference has concluded.

Part IV: Thinking About Assumptions, Again.

What did you notice about the results from the rest of the class?

Why might different groups have come to different conclusions?

Review your assumptions from Part II. Specifically, what are you assuming about the battery in the second circuit?

Think of a situation where the hypothesis could be true even if the result didn't match the prediction.

Think of a situation where the hypothesis could be not true even if the result did match the prediction.

In Part I, we ask students to build a circuit and design an experiment that probes their ability to correlate a hypothesis on electric circuits with a reasonable testing experiment for that hypothesis. As a reminder, student take several approaches to designing a testing experiment when confronted with the student statement in Activity 7.2. Some are good, and some are not so good. Usually, within a group setting, students come up with some variation of the following experiments that we detailed in Chapter 6:

S4: Get a different battery, bulb and set of wires and build a second circuit with the battery in the opposite orientation.

S5: Using the same components, turn the battery in the opposite orientation.

In Part II, we get students to think about the assumptions that they are making using the questions from Thinking Task 7.3. We then hold a short "conference," where representatives from each group describe their IAT statements and their ideas about assumptions made in the design of their testing experiments. Usually, most groups come up with testing experiments similar to either S4 or S5. You will then tell the class that you want to look at the S4 approach. You hand out materials to build a second circuit and the students complete Part III.

Here is what I do: I give half of the groups fully charged batteries and the other half nearly dead batteries. If you do experiments using batteries in your classroom, then you know that there will be a *lot* of nearly dead batteries lying around. What this will do is produce two sets of results:

1. half of the groups will observe no difference in brightness between the two bulbs on their table, supporting the hypothesis, and
2. half of the groups will observe a significant difference in brightness between the two bulbs on their table, not supporting the hypothesis.

Many of your students will (rightfully) believe some sort of shenanigans are happening. Hold another conference where group representatives present their results. Now, the groups have to go back and think about the assumptions that are being made. They must think of a situation where the hypothesis could be true even if the result didn't match the prediction. They also must think of a situation where the hypothesis could be not true even if the result did match the prediction. What they will ultimately determine is that the experiment is based on the assumption that the batteries are identical. If they are not identical, then it has a significant effect on the judgment.

At the end of the activity, I often lead a discussion where we go back to their original ideas for testing experiments and have them think about the S5 approach. In the S5 approach, they have to make significantly less assumptions about the components of the circuit. Because of the relative lack of assumptions being made, we can have more confidence in the results of the experiment.

This activity is an excellent example of a short lesson where you can highlight how assumptions affect science experiments and how we always have to try to identify and think about the assumptions we are making. In fact, the Rutgers University Physics Education Research Group's rubric for assessing testing experiments explicitly includes criteria on identifying assumptions and determining the effect assumptions have on the prediction. Table 7.7 shows an example criterion for assessing the identification of assumptions taken from their larger rubric on testing experiments (Etkina, et al., 2006). I encourage you to see how this criterion fits within the full rubric for assessing testing experiments by looking at the full rubric. The website were all of the rubrics for assessing scientific abilities can be found is provided in the references section below (ISLE Physics Network, 2018).

TABLE 7.7 EXAMPLE CRITERION FOR ASSESSING THE IDENTIFICATION OF ASSUMPTIONS

Ability	Missing	Inadequate	Needs improvement	Adequate
Is able to identify the assumptions made in making the prediction	No attempt is made to identify any assumptions.	An attempt is made to identify assumptions, but the assumptions are irrelevant or confused with the hypothesis.	Relevant assumptions are identified but are not significant for making the prediction.	Sufficient assumptions are correctly identified, and are significant for the prediction that is made.

Source: Etkina, et al., 2006

Summary

In summary, this chapter has been devoted to getting your students to *critically* evaluate their own thinking, their own judgements, and the thinking and judgements of others. Specifically, we discussed the philosophical foundation of metacognition and human cognitive development's role in shaping how it's used. We divided metacognition into two areas:

1. awareness, and
2. regulation.

With respect to metacognition as a science thinking practice, we discussed measurement uncertainty, how assumptions can affect judgements, and the relative value of uncertainty. Specifically, I provided a final set of Thinking Tasks that you can use in your classroom to help ensure students are truly reflecting on their lessons and the level of certainty their results can provide. We revisited two example activities from previous chapters, and learned how to incorporate metacognitive questioning into those examples. This line of questioning is designed to move student views about the validity of science from novice-like to expert-like.

The following is a brief summary of the main points:

◆ Metacognition can be divided into two categories as follows:

  ◇ metacognitive awareness, and
  ◇ metacognitive regulation.

◆ Metacognitive awareness takes the following three forms:

  ◇ declarative awareness,
  ◇ procedural awareness, and
  ◇ conditional awareness.

◆ The three components of metacognitive regulation are as follows:

◇ planning,
◇ monitoring, and
◇ evaluating.

◆ Good metacognition must be developed over time, and metacognitive strategies must be made explicit.

◆ Students view science as a collection of facts, whereas scientists view science as tentative and refutable. This effects the student's ability to evaluate the relative value of evidence.

◆ Scientists think about the relative value of evidence in two ways:

◇ by evaluating measurement uncertainty, and
◇ by evaluating assumptions.

◆ Constant reflection on the relative value of evidence is necessary to move student views about science from novice-like to expert-like.

References

Brown, A. L., & DeLoache, J. S. (1978). Skills, plans, and self-regulation. In R. Siegler (ed.), *Children's thinking: What develops?* (pp. 3–6). Hillsdale, NJ : Lawrence Erlbaum.

Brown, A., Bransford, J., Ferrara, R., & Campione, J. (1983). Learning, remembering, and understanding. In J. H. Flavell, & E. M. Markman (eds), *Handbook of Child Psychology, Vol. 3 Cognitive Development* 4th ed. (pp. 78–166). New York: Wiley.

Brown, J., Collins, A., & Duguid, P. (1989). Situated Cognition and the Culture of Learning. *Educational Researcher, 18*, 32.

Coletta, V. P., & Phillips, J. A. (2005). Interpreting FCI scores: Normalized gain, preinstruction scores, and scientific reasoning ability. *American Journal of Physics, 73*, 1172.

Dewey, J. (1910). *How We Think.* Boston: D.C. Heath Company.

Edmondson, K. M., & Novak, J. D. (1993). The interplay of scientific epistemological views, learning strategies, and attitudes of college students. *Journal of Research in Science Teaching, 30*, 547–559.

Etkina, E., Van Heuvelen, A., White-Brahmia, S., Brookes, D., Gentile, M., Murthy, S., . . . Warren, A. (2006). Scientific abilities and their assessment. *Physical Review ST Physics Education Research, 2*, 020103.

Flavell, J. H. (1979). Metacognition and cognitive monitoring: A new area of cognitive-development inquiry. *American Psychologist, 34*, 906–911.

Flavell, J. H., & Wellman, H. M. (1977). Metamemory. In V. Kail, & J. Hagen (eds), *Perspectives on the Development of Memory and Cognition* (pp. 3–33). Hillsdale, NJ: Lawrence Erlbaum.

Hestenes, I., & Halloun, D. (1998). Interpreting VASS Dimensions and Profiles. *Science & Education, 7*(6), 553–577.

Inhelder, B., & Piaget, J. (1969). *Early Growth of Logic in the Child*. New York, NY: W. W. Norton & Company, Inc.

ISLE Physics Network. (2018, June 27). Retrieved from Investigating Science Learning Environment: www.islephysics.net/

Lawson, A. E., Clark, B., Cramer-Meldrum, E., Falconer, K. A., Sequist, J., & Kwon, Y. (2000). Development of scientific reasoning in college biology: Do two levels of general hypothesis-testing skills exist? *Journal of Research on Science Teaching, 37*, 81.

McRae, M. (2006, March). Educating Future Critical Thinkers. *SWIFT Magazine*.

Moore, C. (2017). *Creating Scientists: Teaching and Assessing Science Practice for the NGSS*. New York, NY: Routledge.

Moore, J. C. (2012). Transitional to Formal Operational: Using Authentic Research Experiences to Get Non-Science Students to Think More Like Scientists. *European Journal of Physics Education, 3*(4), 1–12.

Moore, J. C., & Rubbo, L. J. (2012). Scientific reasoning abilities of nonscience majors in physics-based courses. *Physical Review Special Topics – Physics Education Research, 8*, 010106.

Vygotsky, L. S. (1986). *Thought and language*. (A. Kozulin, Ed.) Cambridge, MA: The MIT Press.

Part III
Putting It All Together

8

Weaving Science Thinking
into Curriculum

"Let the questions be the curriculum."

—Socrates (unknown)

In Part I of this book, we set the foundation for teaching science thinking, where we discussed the specific science thinking patterns, how science thinking is integrated into standards, and the subtle details about effective methods for teaching science thinking. In Part II of this book, we explored each of the science thinking patterns in more detail. I provided you with classroom-ready Thinking Tasks that are specifically designed to be incorporated into any existing lesson or future lesson, and I showed you example activities and assessment strategies for the individual science thinking tasks. In this final chapter, I'm going to describe how to put all of the pieces together. How can you weave science thinking into your curriculum? What does curriculum with science thinking deeply embedded look like?

First, we're going to discuss the curriculum development process in more detail. Specifically, I'm going to describe the two basic theories for curriculum development and suggest a sort of middle ground between the two. I'll then show you where and how you should stick science thinking into activities during this hybrid curriculum development process. We want to make sure that we slowly build thinking abilities when working in new contexts. Some of this will be review from Chapter 3 with a good deal more detail.

Once we have a framework for building a curriculum, I'll go through the entire curriculum development process for one NGSS performance expectation on magnetic fields in middle school physical science. (Remember that the specific content and grade level is an example to clarify the process.) We'll discuss how to define learning goals, weave thinking into the sequence, build the learning experiences, and what to look for in student work as markers for success. We'll use the lessons learned throughout the book, specifically discussing where Thinking Tasks can be placed and how to slowly build science thinking ability in new contexts. Finally, I'll show you how to incorporate experiments into summative assessments and tease out student reasoning to determine what's going on in their minds. As promised in the previous chapter, I will show you an example of how to use Thinking Task 7.1 in an authentic exploration.

Curriculum and Assessment: A Framework for Making It Count

Table 8.1 shows the basic steps for laying out an assessable curriculum, which also serve as a guide for the rest of the chapter. Specifically, to teach and assess science thinking abilities in concert with science practice and content, you will need to do the following:

- ◆ identify learning goals
- ◆ align the curriculum with those goals
- ◆ create both formative and summative assessments

TABLE 8.1 THE BASIC STEPS FOR BUILDING AN ASSESSABLE CURRICULUM

Task	Description
Identify learning goals	What is it that you want the student to understand?
Align curriculum w/ goals	How can you build a curriculum that achieves this understanding?
Create assessments	How will you evaluate whether not the student understands?
Communicate goals	How are you communicating to the student what they are expected to understand by the end of the course/lesson?
Re-evaluate	How will you know if your curriculum is working?

◆ communicate those learning goals to the student
◆ re-evaluate everything based on student feedback and classroom experience.

I would like to point out that the generic framework shown in Table 8.1 is not specific to designing activities and associated assessments in science. In fact, for those of you that are in-service teachers, it should look roughly familiar since it is exactly the same research-based framework we would expect to use for curriculum development in any context.

In particular, when done correctly, the development of assessment and curriculum go hand-in-hand. In order to assess science thinking, you must first know how to build a curriculum that incorporates science thinking. To that end, I'll briefly describe two approaches from the research literature on curriculum development and their implications for assessment: 1. product-based, and 2. process-based curriculum (Smith, 2000). Then, I'll show you how you can use this research to structure your thinking about what to do in your own classes.

The traditional product-based curriculum development theorist Ralph Tyler describes a systematic framework for developing learning, where learning objectives are set, a plan of action is determined and put into place, and the "products" are measured (Tyler, 1949). Curriculum theorist Hilda Taba synthesized a procedure for product-based curriculum development as follows (Taba, 1962):

Step 1: Diagnosis of need
Step 2: Formulation of objectives
Step 3: Selection of content
Step 4: Organization of content
Step 5: Selection of learning experiences
Step 6: Organization of learning experiences
Step 7: Determination of what to evaluate and of the ways and means of doing it.

This procedure looks very similar to the shorter steps shown in Table 8.1, with the obvious omission of the final reflective step. However, we must be careful with taking strict procedural approaches to the practice of teaching. In particular, when we set the entire curriculum including assessments before day one of instruction, we leave the learner out of the process all together. They participate in activities we design, but they have little say in the actual learning process. Furthermore, feedback they provide via assessments play no role in future instruction. This approach also has the effect of forcing a focus on the individual "products" themselves, instead of a consistent learning experience, which can minimize learning that happens outside of pre-defined products.

As an example, imagine our product is the following NGSS performance expectation (we'll come back to this example in later sections, too):

MS-PS2–5. Conduct an investigation and evaluate the experimental design to provide evidence that fields exist between objects exerting forces on each other even though the objects are not in contact.

A significant amount of learning has to happen leading up to a student being able to demonstrate understanding in the domain of magnetic fields. Maybe a student would develop a taxonomy of materials, including magnetic, ferromagnetic, and non-magnetic materials. How do these different types of materials interact with each other? They might discover that not all metals are ferromagnetic. What "makes" a magnet? What's a compass? All of these ideas would be built into activities leading up to a field model for magnetic interactions. Much of this learning isn't explicitly mentioned in the NGSS. Is this learning less important? If not, then do we just need to add more and more performance expectations to cover everything?

The practical effect of curriculum as products is the breaking down of learning into smaller and smaller units, where the teacher is faced with an avalanche of stuff to teach and assess and little to no flexibility. More recent research shows that curriculums based on products, or strict "learning objectives," are rarely actually implemented in this way, anyway (Cornbleth, 1990). This isn't necessarily a failure of the teacher, but possibly a failure of the framework to align with how learning actually happens. There are interesting parallels between the practice of science and the practice of teaching. The *Framework* and NGSS on which this entire book is written fundamentally lay out science as a process to be practiced. Similarly, the research in curriculum development is also beginning to focus on teaching as a process to be practiced.

Process-based curriculum recognizes learning as an interaction between the teacher and the student, with learning happening in both directions (Stenhouse, 1975). The focus is more on big ideas where the curriculum *is* the interaction, allowing for a more organic learning experience. With respect to the NGSS, the set of DCIs is significantly smaller than would be typical for more "traditional" science standards. Within the NGSS, the main focus is on the interaction between the practices, content, and cross-cutting ideas (the science thinking). This has the practical benefit of having less "stuff" to assess, and when implemented correctly, allows greater flexibility on how that interaction is taught and learned, allowing freedom for student input into the curriculum.

In her book *Curriculum: Product or Praxis?*, Shirley Grundy describes process-based curriculum as follows (Grundy, 1987):

> *Critical pedagogy goes beyond situating the learning experience within the experience of the learner: it is a process which takes the experiences of both the learner and the teacher and, through dialogue and negotiation, recognizes them both as problematic.*

Doing science and thinking about science necessitates negotiation between everyone involved, including both the teacher and the student. It makes sense, then, that we would want to more thoroughly involve our students in the science learning, and even curriculum building processes. Furthermore, we as teachers must accept this two-way negotiation, and recognize that the feedback we get from the student can help us better teach them.

In particular, with respect to science, students enter the classroom with their own experiences and mental models for the world around them based on those experiences. Sometimes, their experiences lead to mental models that clash with "correct" models of the world. Specifically, in the mind of the student, the idea that the squished bug on the windshield exerted the same force on the car as the car exerted on it is preposterous. No matter how much we tell the student otherwise, they won't believe us, whether or not they can regurgitate the "fact" on a test.

If we wish to lead them to understanding, we cannot discount these experiences and pre-existing mental models. Their ideas are valid, even if based on limited experiences. In this example, the student has a *different* model in their mind for force, and it isn't an absurd model based on their experiences. The bug *lost*! We must learn from the student how they think and why they think that way, so that we can build learning experiences that lead the student to grow without having to invalidate their own experiences. Sometimes, as teachers, we can anticipate the students' thinking, and sometimes we cannot. When we can't, we need to readjust our own teaching if necessary, and even re-evaluate our learning goals from time to time. This is curriculum as process.

We have to be careful here, though. More than likely the state you work in, and/or the school system in which you teach, has some pretty specific ideas about what your students should be learning. Within the confines of formal schooling, there is only so much leverage the student has in negotiating learning goals, if any. The NGSS has defined performance expectations that you will have to assess, no matter how many great arguments your students make. There is a great deal of flexibility, but there is also a definite structure.

This is why Table 8.1 takes a hybrid approach to curriculum development, where we are systematic about our goals and the process we go through to develop activities, but we leave open the ability to re-evaluate our own teaching and curriculum decisions based on feedback from students. We have a well-defined plan, but we recognize the need for occasional flexibility. For example, we may have a performance expectation like MS-PS2–5 discussed above, but we have a great deal of flexibility in how we build a learning progression that gets everyone there, and we have the freedom to go beyond strictly delineated products in the design of that progression.

For the rest of this chapter, we will look at the NGSS as our set of broad-based learning goals and learn to build a curriculum off of these goals using this hybrid approach. To review what we briefly discussed in Chapter 3, Figure 8.1 shows a schematic diagram of the NGSS-based

Figure 8.1 Schematic diagram of a hybrid product/process approach to curriculum development using the NGSS as a guide to defining learning goals

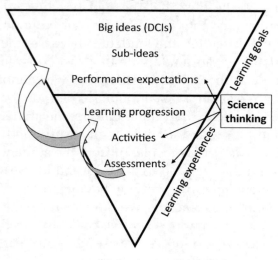

curriculum development process you can use for building your courses, and follows the framework from Table 8.1. You should notice that Figure 8.1 looks like a funnel, because we get more and more detail and more and more specific as we move down the list.

We start out with the big ideas, break these into smaller sub-ideas, and develop broad performance expectations from these sub-ideas. This sets up our set of learning goals. Then, we decide on a learning progression that could lead a student towards understanding demonstrated by the performance expectation. We create specific activities within that progression, and then we assess performance in those activities. All of these items form the overall learning experience for the student. The arrows in the figure represent the "re-evaluate" task from Table 8.1. Occasionally, we learn during assessment that the activities failed miserably to foster understanding, or that the learning progression was missing pieces. In some cases, assessment can lead us to develop completely new goals.

For those of us teaching in the context of well-defined standards such as the NGSS, the first part of the process is done for us. The NGSS have a clearly laid out set of performance expectations for each grade level and disciplinary area. The complicated part, the part you the teacher are now responsible for, is developing the learning experiences and assessments that build students up to these performance expectations. Doing this successfully requires deep discipline-based understanding on the part of the teacher in combination with knowledge and practice in science education methods. This integration of content with content-specific pedagogy is what we call *pedagogical content knowledge* (PCK) (Ball & McDiarmid, 1990; Shulman, 1987). You need to know where the student is starting with respect to content (and doing/thinking!), where you want them to go, what it takes to get them there, what concepts they need to build an understanding, and how to assess whether or not they are progressing.

Unfortunately, this is too small a book to go into great detail on PCK in all sub-disciplines, or even just one. I will provide you a specific example with magnetism, though, to provide an example of how to use PCK in the curriculum development process. The principles are generative, so you should still be able to use the framework and your own knowledge and years of experience in your discipline and with your students to do the same in your domain.

Figure 8.1 also shows you approximately where to consider incorporating science thinking when designing curriculum. As discussed in Chapter 2, we find science thinking littered throughout the performance expectations of the NGSS, even when they aren't explicit. Therefore, science thinking and the minimum set of six patterns we have identified throughout the book are components of our learning goals. Since thinking is ultimately something we do in the moment, we don't necessarily include the thinking patterns within our development of a learning progression. However, when students are in action, those thinking abilities will be on full display. It is at the activity and assessment levels that we need to build in explicit instruction on science thinking, reflective discussions, and formative and summative tests of thinking ability.

Identifying What We Want Students to Learn: An Example from Physical Science

To demonstrate the hybrid approach to curriculum development and how to incorporate science thinking into it, let's imagine that we're building a curriculum for middle school physical science. I also want you to imagine that you are doing this in an NGSS state. To determine our learning target, we'll first look at the big ideas we want students to learn, then we'll break those big ideas down into manageable sub-ideas, and then determine specific performance expectations we have for students on each of those sub-ideas (as outlined in Figure 8.1). The performance expectations serve as our learning goals and as the foundation of any resulting activities and assessments.

Table 8.2 shows the middle school physical science DCIs from the NGSS with corresponding sub-ideas (NGSS Lead States, 2013b). At the beginning of the academic year when we start thinking about our curriculum, we begin by looking at these four big ideas in physical science. Specifically, the physical science ideas that carry through the grade levels in the NGSS are:

1. matter and its interactions,
2. forces,
3. energy, and
4. waves.

Each of the DCIs can be broken down into multiple sub-ideas. Table 8.2 also shows the specific sub-ideas with the associated performance expectations for *forces and interactions* shown in Table 8.3 (NGSS Lead States,

TABLE 8.2 MIDDLE SCHOOL PHYSICAL SCIENCE DCIS FROM THE NGSS

	Disciplinary core ideas	**Sub-ideas**
MS-PS1	Matter and its Interactions	Structure of matter Chemical reactions
MS-PS2	Forces and Interactions	Forces and motion Types of interactions Stability and instability
MS-PS3	Energy	Definitions of energy Conservation of energy Energy and forces Energy in chemical reactions
MS-PS4	Waves	Wave properties Electromagnetic radiation Information technology

Source: NGSS Lead States, 2013b

TABLE 8.3 PERFORMANCE EXPECTATIONS FOR DCI MS-PS2, FORCES AND INTERACTIONS

	Performance Expectations
MS-PS2–1	Apply Newton's Third Law to *design a solution to a problem* involving the motion of two colliding objects.
MS-PS2–2	*Plan an investigation* to provide evidence that the change in an object's motion depends on the sum of the forces on the object and the mass of the object.
MS-PS2–3	*Ask questions* about data to determine the factors that affect the strength of electric and magnetic forces.
MS-PS2–4	*Construct and present arguments using evidence* to support the claim that gravitational interactions are attractive and depend on the masses of interacting objects.
MS-PS2–5	*Conduct an investigation* and evaluate the experimental design to provide evidence that fields exist between objects exerting forces on each other even though the objects are not in contact.

Source: Adapted from NGSS Lead States, 2013b

2013b). At the middle school level, we're interested in students learning about the role of the mass of an object and how it can be qualitatively accounted for in changes of motion due to forces. Furthermore, we want students to understand field models of forces, and how fields can be mapped by relative strength and effect on objects. As can be seen from the performance expectations, we define understanding through the student's ability to practice science in these specific content domains. Looking way back at Figure 2.2, you can also see how the science thinking patterns will be necessary to perform these practices.

A large-view map of content and its progression throughout the grade levels for each discipline can be found in *Appendix E: Progressions Within the Next Generation Science Standard* (NGSS Lead States, 2013b). When beginning the development of your own curriculum, this is an excellent place to start. I recommend going through the appendix and building your own set of tables similar to Tables 8.2 and 8.3, where one table lays out the big picture (similar to Table 8.2), and several other tables drill down on the specific ideas to address in the classroom through the performance expectations (similar to Table 8.3).

Designing Learning Experiences: An Example from Magnetism

The DCIs and performance expectations set our goals for learning. In the last section, we used the NGSS to build a map that started with big ideas we want students to understand and narrowed down to specific performance expectations that can demonstrate understanding of those ideas. However, defining what we want students to understand is not yet a complete curriculum. We now must begin to think about the specific learning experiences we want students to go through in the classroom that can lead to the understanding that we seek.

Let's revisit the performance expectation for magnetic fields that we discussed earlier and found in Table 8.3:

MS-PS2–5. *Conduct an investigation* and evaluate the experimental design to provide evidence that fields exist between objects exerting forces on each other even though the objects are not in contact.

This performance expectation centers on the science practice of designing and conducting investigations. Looking back at Figure 2.2, we see that the practice of planning an investigation requires the science thinking patterns of causative thinking, control of variables, and hypothetical-deductive thinking. Therefore, at a minimum, we will need to incorporate these thinking tasks into our learning progression.

The natural tendency based on a product-view of curriculum would be to immediately begin creating an activity and assessment for this individual performance expectation. However, as we have already discussed, a significant amount of learning has to happen before we can expect the student to understand a concept as abstract as an invisible field. Some of this learning could be built into the K–5 curriculum, but not all of it. We need to build a learning progression that guides the student towards a field model of the magnetic force, and ideally revisits learning from previous grade levels.

I want to highlight that I know roughly what this progression should look like from decades of experience and explicit training in PCK within the discipline of physics. Most of the sequence I'm about to show you actually comes from adaptation of the University of Washington Physics Education Group's book *Physics by Inquiry* (McDermott, 1996). I wish I could claim that teacher preparation programs and disciplinary departments in our universities prepare you well to do this on your own, but we are all unfortunately behind where we need to be with teaching this specific knowledge teachers need (Etkina, 2010). As an example, physics professors are notorious for offering physics courses that look nothing like what we would want the K–12 classroom to look like. Knowing how to build a learning progression is the hardest part of this process. Don't let that discourage you. So long as you continually reflect on your teaching and your students' learning, you will learn what works and what doesn't through time.

Table 8.4 shows an example of a possible learning progression for magnets that could lead to an understanding of magnetic fields and more. We start with magnetic interactions, build on that by using compasses to develop a field model for the magnetic force, and then cap learning by exploring magnetic strength based on stacking magnets in various orientations. I have also listed a basic description of the types of activities that

TABLE 8.4 EXAMPLE LEARNING PROGRESSION FOR MAGNETS

Ideas	Science thinking patterns	Activities
Magnets and interaction	Pattern recognition Metacognitive awareness	Taxonomy of interactions for materials What is different about a magnet and a ferromagnet? Are all metals magnetic? Close your eyes, can you tell which object is the magnet?
Abstract models: magnetic fields	Pattern recognition Causative thinking Control of variables Hypothetical-deductive thinking Metacognitive awareness	A field model for magnets from compass needles – developing a model Arrangements of magnets and magnetic strength – using a model
Exploration: magnetic strength	Causative thinking Control of variables Hypothetical-deductive thinking Metacognitive regulation Metacognitive awareness	Designing an experiment to measure the strength of magnets Stacking magnets How does it fit the model we have for magnetic interactions?

could be done along with the specific science thinking patterns that would be used during these activities. This serves as a guide to inserting the Thinking Tasks into the curriculum.

We have already discussed an activity to develop understanding of magnetic interactions in Activity 4.2. For review, Figure 8.2 shows a student developing a taxonomy of magnetic materials categorized by their interactions with each other. In this particular activity, we used similarly shaped un-marked rods made of different materials that the students played with to discover the various types of interactions. Activity 4.2 used the questions from Thinking Task 4.1 on pattern recognition.

We use a series of informal observations, formal observation experiments, and testing experiments with compasses to develop a model for magnetic fields. For example, Figure 8.3 shows a student having marked the direction of a compass as it was moved around a magnet. In this particular activity, the student must recognize a pattern in the way that the

Figure 8.2 Example of student work sorting cylinders based on magnetic interactions

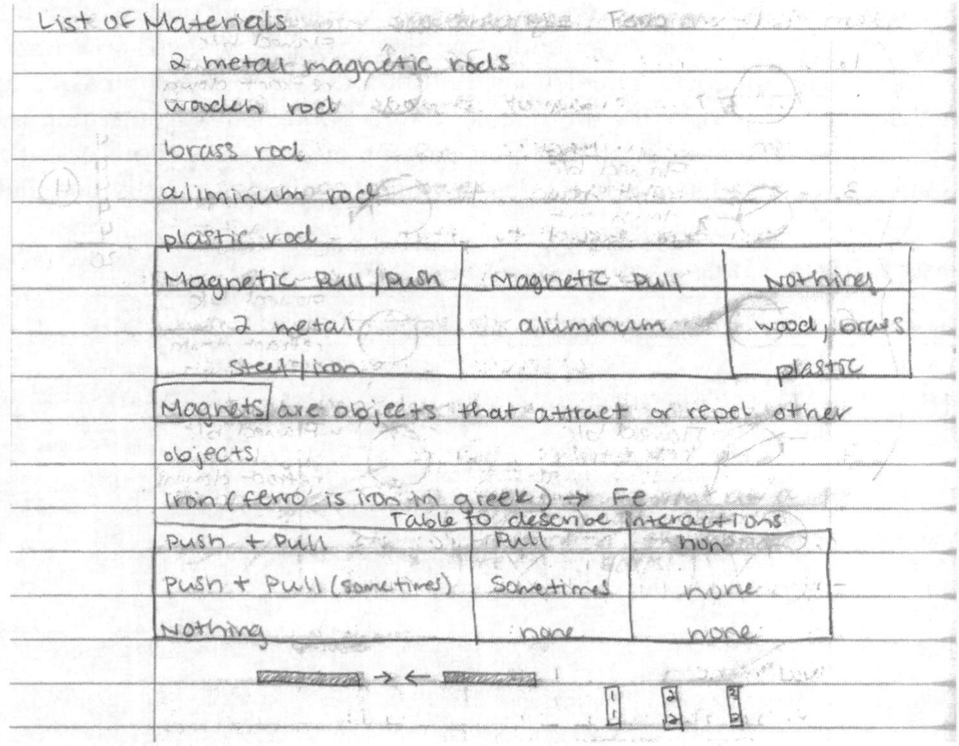

Figure 8.3 Example of student work investigating the magnetic field around a magnet using compasses

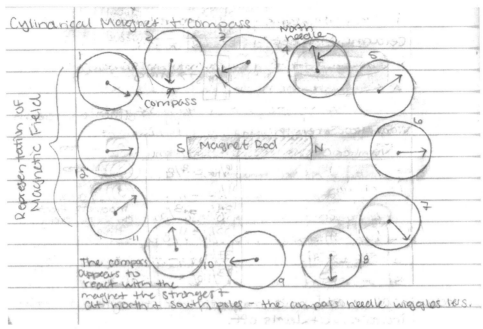

compass behaves so that they can begin to generalize a phenomenological model. This also requires basic causative thinking.

Figure 8.4 shows a similar activity using multiple magnets, where the student made a prediction using the field model and then they tested that prediction. Activities leading up to this one might have the students investigating how the compass behaves when in between two magnets and what happens as magnets are moved away from the compass. You can see at the top of Figure 8.4 that the student is articulating a predictive model for compass behavior when confronted with more than one magnet (termed "superposition" in the notebook). The development of this predictive model required a bunch of science thinking patterns and the hypothesis-generation process we discussed in Chapters 4 and 5. The bottom of Figure 8.4 shows the student making a prediction based on their model and then sketching the results of the actual experiment. This requires hypothetical-deductive thinking.

Notice that at all stages, the questions and worksheets from the Thinking Tasks can be used. Furthermore, the Thinking Tasks on metacognitive awareness (measurement uncertainty and thinking about assumptions)

Figure 8.4 Example of student work testing a model for magnetic fields. The student can be seen articulating the model, making a prediction based on the model for a certain new situation, and then testing to see if the prediction comes true

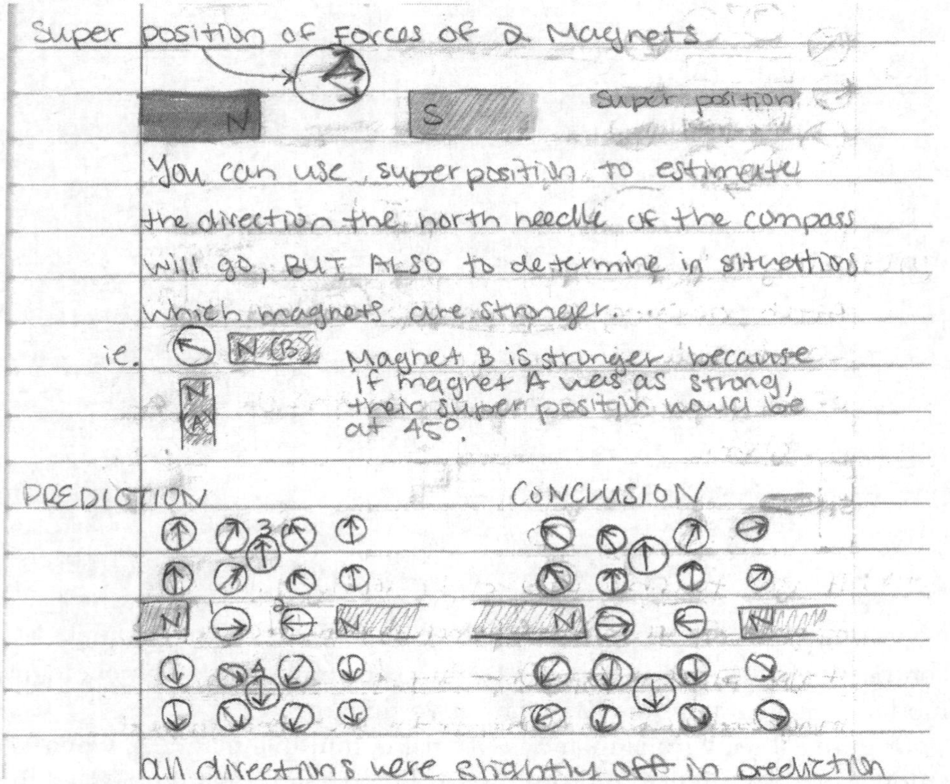

can be utilized to help shift student views about science away from novice-like views and towards expert-like views.

Some of the content in the learning progression shown in Table 8.4 can be explicitly found in the NGSS, while some is nowhere to be seen. For example, in the 3rd grade, magnetic interactions are discussed, as evidenced by the following performance expectation (NGSS Lead States, 2013b):

> 3-PS2–3.   Ask questions to determine cause and effect relationships of electric or magnetic interactions between two objects not in contact with each other.

Students ask questions about magnetic force between two permanent magnets, and/or the force between a magnet and paperclips, and/or the strength of the force exerted by one magnet versus two magnets stacked together. Magnets don't explicitly re-appear in the NGSS until the middle school performance expectation we're using as our example. There is no explicit performance expectation for students using a model for magnetic fields to make predictions about the orientation of a compass needle between multiple magnets, as seen in Figure 8.4. That doesn't mean that such an activity is unnecessary. It certainly provides evidence for the existence of fields!

Often misunderstood, the NGSS is a *minimum* set of standards and *not* curriculum. Performance expectations are big-view goals and not products. It's perfectly acceptable and even necessary to expand on both the content and practices described in the NGSS, especially if it helps strengthen student understanding about a topic. If you want to teach science thinking, then I've shown from the research that it will be absolutely critical that you incorporate explicit instruction, even if there is no formal dictate in the standards. Understanding requires knowing, doing, and thinking, so thinking is going to have to make its way into your curriculum, anyway.

It's important for students to utilize as many science practices and science thinking patterns as possible throughout the learning cycle. For example, in the learning progression on magnets that I've shown you in Table 8.4, students ask questions, develop and use models, conduct investigations, analyze data, use mathematics, construct explanations, argue from evidence, and communicate information, all on the singular topic of magnets. Furthermore, they use all six science thinking patterns and every one of the explicit Thinking Tasks we've discuss in this book.

Your classroom instruction is not and should not be confined to *only* gathering evidence for fields because that's all the NGSS asks. There are two problems with such a simple approach: 1. students aren't prepared for magnetic fields without deep understanding of magnetic interactions, and 2. students need to see and practice doing and thinking as much as possible. When they go through the entire scientific method I laid out in Figure 1.3 on one piece of content (in this case magnetism), and then do the same thing for the next piece of content, they begin to better understand the crosscutting nature of the practices and thinking patterns.

At the end of the learning progression, the student is prepared for the NGSS performance expectation. They now understand magnetism through multiple levels, having practiced and thought about magnets scientifically from many different perspectives. They will also now be familiar with assessment, since you will have formatively assessed their work in a low-stakes manner throughout the learning progression using rubrics and assessment items like I've discussed in Part II of this book. Any summative assessment based on the performance expectation would be similar.

Summative Assessment of Doing and Thinking: An Example from Stacking Magnets

Now that we've laid a foundation in magnetism, we can allow students to independently explore on the topic and ultimately see how they handle the performance expectation. Eventually, we must raise the stakes and administer tests that summatively assess each student's individual abilities. As mentioned, your summative assessments should look similar to your formative assessments. With this in mind, we can look back at how we formatively assessed science practice in context, and use these same principles to summatively assess the individual.

Activity 8.1 shows an example of an activity-based test and the corresponding rubric that would be used to score the test. In this particular test, we have the students plan and conduct an investigation on the affect stacking magnets has on the magnitude of the force. Students are provided a very limited set of materials that they are allowed to use in their investigation.

Activity 8.1 Summative Assessment for Conducting an Investigation on Magnetic Strength

In this activity, you will individually plan and conduct an experiment that determines how the strength of the magnetic force depends on the number of magnets stacked in a stable configuration. You will be provided with five un-marked, circular magnets, several paperclips, and a ruler. You may use only these items to conduct the experiment. All work must be recorded in your scientific notebook.

In addition to documenting your planning and experimental execution in your scientific notebook, complete the worksheet for Thinking Task 7.1 before (planning), during (monitoring), and after (evaluating) the activity.

Your work will be graded based on the following rubric:

Identifies the phenomenon to be investigated			
	Unsatisfactory	**Needs improvement**	**Satisfactory**
Identifies the phenomenon under investigation.	The student makes no attempt to identify the phenomenon.	The student identifies the phenomenon, but it is the incorrect phenomenon or is unclear.	The student clearly identifies the correct phenomenon based on the plan.
Identifies the purpose of the investigation.	The student makes no attempt to identify the purpose of the investigation.	The student makes an attempt to identify the purpose, but it is unclear.	The student clearly identifies the purpose of the investigation.

Identifies evidence to address the purpose of the investigation			
	Unsatisfactory	**Needs improvement**	**Satisfactory**
Develops an investigation plan that describes the data to be collected.	The student makes no attempt to describe the data to be collected.	The student makes an attempt to describe the data to be collected, but it is unclear or does not distinguish the variables.	The student describes the data that will be collected, including independent and dependent variables.
Develops an investigation plan that describes the evidence to be derived from the data.	The student makes no attempt to describe the evidence to be derived from the data.	The student makes an attempt to describe that evidence, but it is unclear or the proposed evidence cannot answer the research question.	The student described the evidence to be derived from the data, including how the data will be used to answer the research question.

Plans the investigation			
	Unsatisfactory	**Needs improvement**	**Satisfactory**
Describes how the magnetic force will be measured with the available equipment.	The student does not describe how the magnetic force will be measured.	The student describes how the magnetic force will be measured, but the measurement either can't be done with the materials provided, or will not result in measuring the magnetic force.	The student describes how the magnetic force will be measured and it will result in a useful measurement.
Control of variables: Is able to decide what physical quantities are to be measured and identify independent and dependent variables.	Only some of the physical quantities are relevant.	The physical quantities are relevant. However, independent and dependent variables are not identified.	The physical quantities are relevant and independent and dependent variables are identified.

Collects the data			
	Unsatisfactory	**Needs improvement**	**Satisfactory**
Makes and records observations according to the given plan.	No observations are recorded.	Observations are recorded, but not based on the given plan OR observations are incorrectly recorded OR the record is unclear.	Observations are recorded clearly and in accordance with the given plan.
Relative value of evidence: Is able to identify measurement uncertainties.	No measurement uncertainties are identified.	Most measurement uncertainties are not identified.	All measurement uncertainties are identified.
Analyzes the data			
	Unsatisfactory	**Needs improvement**	**Satisfactory**
Makes a graph that shows how the magnetic force depends on the number of magnets.	No graph is provided	A graph is provided, but does not display the collected data OR is improperly labeled OR is not labeled at all.	A graph is provided that properly displays the collected data AND is correctly labeled.
Pattern recognition: Is able to identify a pattern in the data.	The pattern described is irrelevant or inconsistent with the data.	The pattern has minor errors. Terms such as proportional are used without clarity. Is the proportionality linear, etc.	The pattern described represents the relevant trend in the data.

The rubric is attached and provided to the student before the test. Furthermore, the rubric has the same structure as the rubrics used during the regular class time. Therefore, the expectations are not only clear, but the student should have had the opportunity to practice meeting those same expectations in different contexts. I have highlighted some of the science thinking criteria (bold and underlined) used previously in the book to show you an example of how these criteria can be placed into rubrics. If you have read my previous book *Creating Scientists*, you already know how to use the NGSS evidence statements to assess science practice, which is also demonstrated in the rubric (NGSS Lead States, 2013a; Moore, 2017).

Figure 8.5 shows a partial example of student work on the activity-based test shown in Activity 8.1. In this sample of student work, we see the student's recorded data and can get an idea of how they decided to measure the magnetic force. This student used the ruler to measure how

Figure 8.5 Example of recorded data from a student exam on conducting an investigation to determine the effect of stacking magnets on the magnetic strength

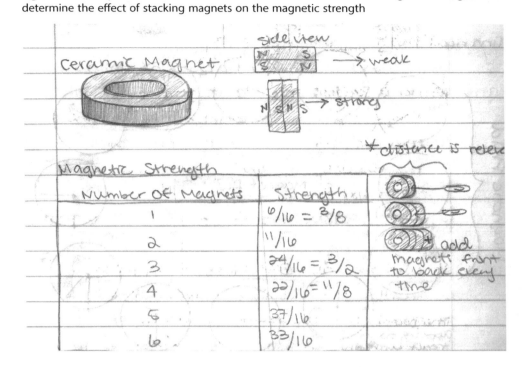

far away the paperclip needed to rest before being attracted to the face of the magnet. The force measurement is being made in units of fractions of inches. The student can then plot the force as a function of the number of magnets (not shown).

You will actually be amazed at how readily students come up with ingenious ways to make measurements with limited amounts of materials. The natural tendency is to reach for a "magnetic force meter," but no such device really exists. You'll also be amazed at how much students enjoy being tested in this manner. It's not *really* a test. They're playing!

There are several keys to good activity-based tests. First, they should be relatively short and simple activities. The materials also need to be small and plentiful. In our case, it is easy for a student to work as an individual at their desk using a few small magnets, paperclips, and a ruler. However, if we instead attempted to have them roll bowling balls down the hall and measure speed, then that would be impractical for any normal size class. It might make an excellent group activity, but a terrible activity-based test.

Summary

In summary, we've looked at developing curriculum that incorporates the assessment of science thinking in context. I described the two basic theories for curriculum development and presented a middle ground between the two. I then showed you where and how to incorporate science thinking into activities during this hybrid curriculum development process. To demonstrate the process, I showed you an example curriculum developed for one NGSS performance expectation on magnetic fields in middle school physical science. You learned how to define learning goals, weave thinking into the sequence, build the learning experiences, and what to look for in student work as markers for success. Finally, I showed you how to incorporate experiments into summative assessments and tease out student thinking in rubrics to determine what's going on in their minds.

The following is a brief summary of the main points:

◆ Curriculum is best thought of as a process, as opposed to a series of products.
◆ NGSS performance expectations can be used to define learning goals.

In designing a learning progression that achieves our learning goals, we must go beyond the NGSS. Just because content isn't in the NGSS, or because a certain practice or thinking pattern isn't used with some specific content, doesn't mean we can't use it in our classes. Sometimes we must!

◆ Incorporate science thinking assessment into activity assessment rubrics.
◆ NGSS evidence statements provide a useful foundation for writing practice-based rubric criteria.
◆ If we're going to have students do science during class time, then we should do our best to test them in the same way: by having them do science. Activity-based tests allow for the assessment of practices and content while having the added benefit of being fun.

References

Ball, D. L., & McDiarmid, G. W. (1990). The subject matter preparation of teachers. In W. R. Houston, M. Haberman, & J. Sikula, *Handbook of Research on Teacher Education* (pp. 437–449). New York: Macmillan.

Cornbleth, C. (1990). *Curriculum in Context.* Basingstoke: Falmer Press.

Etkina, E. (2010). Pedagogical Content Knowledge and Preparation of High School Physics Teachers. *Physical Review Special Topics – Physics Education Research, 6*(2).

Grundy, S. (1987). *Curriculum: Product or Praxis?* New York: Falmer Press.

McDermott, L. C. (1996). *Physics by Inquiry.* New York: John Wiley & Sons.

Moore, C. (2017). *Creating Scientists: Teaching and Assessing Science Practice for the NGSS.* New York, NY: Routledge.

NGSS Lead States. (2013a). *Evidence Statements.* Retrieved from Next Generation Science Standards: www.nextgenscience.org

NGSS Lead States. (2013b). *Next Generation Science Standards: For States, By States.* Washington, DC: The National Academies Press.

Shulman, L. S. (1987). Knowledge and teaching: Foundations of the new reform. *Harvard Educational Review, 57*, 1–22.

Smith, M. K. (2000). *Curriculum Theory and Practice.* Retrieved from *The Encyclopedia of Informal Education*: www.infed.org/biblio/b-curric.htm

Stenhouse, L. (1975). *An Introduction to Curriculum Research and Development.* London: Heinemann.

Taba, H. (1962). *Curriculum Development: Theory and Practice.* New York: Harcourt Brace and World.

Tyler, R. W. (1949). *Basic Principles of Curriculum and Instruction.* Chicago: University of Chicago Press.